QUICK AND EASY
PASTA
RECIPES

Coleen and Bob Simmons

BRISTOL PUBLISHING ENTERPRISES

San Leandro, California

A **nitty gritty**® Cookbook

Printed in the United States of America.

ISBN: 1-55867-271-0

Cover design:	Frank J. Paredes
Cover photography:	John A. Benson
Food stylist:	Susan Devaty
Illustrator:	Joan Baakkonen

CONTENTS

PASTA — IT'S EATING AT ITS BEST

Enjoy pasta often with a clear conscience — it's good for you! Pasta is one of America's favorite dishes because it is a satisfying, wholesome food, not high in calories. It can be prepared quickly and in many different ways and combined with a wide variety of other healthful foods. A satisfying portion of pasta (about 2 ounces of dried pasta or 3 ounces of fresh pasta before cooking) has slightly more than 200 calories before the addition of a sauce or seasoning. The seasonings can be very pungent because the taste moderates when mixed with the blandness of pasta. Assertive ingredients such as garlic, strong cheese, anchovies and hot peppers can be used in small amounts to give pasta a delicious flavor without adding excessive calories.

In the pages that follow, you'll find information about ingredients, directions for making homemade pasta, and recipes for pasta dishes using fresh seasonal vegetables. Fast, delicious sauces, inventive salad combinations, pasta with meats, easy home made ravioli and new twists on baked pasta dishes will tempt you. If you are like us, you'll never tire of pasta — it's eating at its best.

THE RIGHT INGREDIENTS

ABOUT DRIED PASTA

All dried pastas are of similar composition. They contain hard durum wheat, sometimes with the addition of egg and possibly flavoring or coloring ingredients. There is a wide variation in the "bite" in pastas, even between those made only of wheat and water. The very best pastas tend to be those imported from Italy, with some brands being vastly superior to others. The brands available vary from region to region, so the best approach is to try two or three of the Italian pastas and decide which is best. Two of our favorites brands are Delverde and Latini. A high quality pasta will keep its pale yellow color during cooking, and the cooking water will not become cloudy. Start with one variety, such as linguine, and try it with a simple sauce that really lets the wheaty flavor of the pasta shine through. When you find a brand that pleases you, stick with it and work your way through their various shapes.

There are myriad shapes, colors and flavors of dried pastas from which to choose. Dried lasagna noodles are available that no longer have to be precooked, just layered with sauce and cheese and then microwaved or baked to perfection. There are specialty pastas made of other grains than wheat for people on restricted diets.

ABOUT FRESH PASTA

Supermarket and deli cases today carry spectacular arrays of fresh pasta shapes and ready-to-heat-and-eat sauces. Fresh lasagna noodles are sold by the pound, ready to be cooked, layered with cheese and sauce and baked. Ravioli, tortellini and agnolotti are filled with tasty stuffings. Tomato sauces come thin, thick, or chunky; and with or without meat. If you have the time, excellent fresh pasta can be made at home; we have included instructions and recipes for making your own.

You will find that you prefer certain pasta shapes with specific sauces. Light, delicate sauces tend to go better with thinner pastas. Hearty full-flavored sauces need more substantial pastas. Generally, dried pasta is best for making salads and serving with uncooked sauces because it has more "bite." Fresh egg pastas become soft and mushy in salad preparations, but are wonderful with any sauce based on butter and cream.

Extra virgin olive oils, olive pastes, sun-dried tomatoes either dry or packed in oil, and fresh herbs make quick pasta flavorings. Pesto, garlic puree, olive paste, anchovy paste and sun-dried tomato paste are available in squeeze tubes for times when you need only a tablespoon or two, and keep well in the refrigerator.

ABOUT OLIVE OILS

Wonderful olive oils come from Italy, Spain, France, Greece and California. They range in color from pale yellow to deep green. Oils from Tuscany are elegant and peppery; Greek, Spanish and Sicilian olive oils tend to be more robust and full-flavored. Olive variety, climate and soil all contribute to the unique character of the oil. Olive oil has a limited shelf life after opening, so buy small bottles of several different brands until you find the ones you prefer. You definitely want to have at least one full-flavored, extra virgin olive oil and one or two virgin or pure olive oils on hand. Store olive oil in a cool, dark place, but not in the refrigerator.

Extra virgin oils are cold pressed and retain a wonderful fruity character that is lost in the processing of virgin and other types of oils.

Extra virgin oils are not generally used for heavy frying because they lose fragrance and charm when heated to a high temperature. A few drops of extra virgin olive oil drizzled over a finished plate of hot pasta adds a wonderful touch.

ABOUT TOMATOES

The preferred fresh tomato for use in pasta sauces is the Romano or Italian. It is slightly oval, about the size of a very large egg, and has thick flesh and very few seeds, but any perfectly ripe tomato, which has been peeled and seeded, can be used. If ripe, full-flavored tomatoes are not available, buy a good brand of canned whole Italian plum tomatoes, preferably packed in rich tomato juice, or canned ready-cut tomatoes in juice.

Unless you have a great surplus of tomatoes, there is no reason to start with fresh tomatoes for sauces that require long simmering. The end result is little different from a sauce made with canned tomato sauce or tomato paste.

If you are using whole canned tomatoes, hold the tomato over a sieve which has been set in a small bowl. With a small knife, cut out the hard stem end and discard. Cut tomatoes in half lengthwise and gently squeeze to remove most of the seeds. After all the tomatoes have been seeded, pour the juice remaining in the can through the sieve. If the recipe does not call for the tomato juice, reserve it for another purpose. Chop the tomatoes and add to the sauce you are making at the last minute to preserve their best color and texture.

ABOUT PEPPERS

The distinctive taste of peppers — whether they are red, green, yellow, orange, mild or hot, fresh or dried, cooked or raw — complements the bland taste and smooth texture of pasta very well. The Italians often add a few red pepper flakes to a simmering sauce, or sprinkle a few flakes over a completed dish. Your taste will have to determine the amount used.

Many recipes call for fresh bell peppers. Fresh peppers can be used without peeling, but most recipes will be greatly improved if the peppers are peeled. The very best way to peel a pepper is to cut the pepper into quarters along the natural depressions and peel it with a sharp vegetable peeler. Then remove the seeds and ribs, and cut the pepper in the desired fashion. Peeled peppers cook more rapidly, stay crisper and tend to be easier on sensitive digestive systems.

Roasting peppers to peel them produces a softer, partially cooked pepper. Start by placing the pepper under the broiler or over a barbecue fire or gas flame. Turn frequently to char all sides. When the skin is well blistered, place under a bowl or in a plastic bag and steam for about 15 minutes. The skin will soften and will pull off easily. Do not rinse the roasted peppers under running water. Discard stem and seeds, and cut the peeled pepper in the desired fashion. Roasted peppers can be stored in the refrigerator for several days, or they can be frozen for future use.

ABOUT CHEESES

The very best hard cheese to grate over pasta is aged Italian Parmigiano-Reggiano. It is dry but not grainy and the flavor is assertive, but not sharp. Not only does it taste better, but it is also more economical if you buy Parmigiano by the piece at a good Italian delicatessen or specialty cheese shop and grate it fresh as needed. Hard cheeses grate easily with the microplane-style graters. A whole piece of cheese, well wrapped, can be kept for months in the freezer or several weeks in the refrigerator.

Another Italian cheese often used with pasta is pecorino Romano, which is made from sheep's milk. It has a much more robust flavor than Parmesan and tends to be saltier.

There are other aged cheeses that are properly dry and mellow for grating over pasta. Aged provolone, Gouda, dry Monterey Jack, Asiago, sapsago, and manchego cheeses all work well when grated fresh over pasta. Some markets feature good quality freshly grated cheese in convenient small containers. The grated cheese sold in shaker-top cans in supermarkets may be adequate for use in sauces, but should only be used as a last resort for sprinkling over pasta.

Crumbled feta, mascarpone, fresh mozzarella or fresh goat cheeses are excellent for tossing with hot pasta, to make a quick creamy sauce.

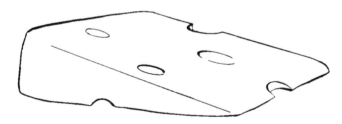

MAKING YOUR OWN PASTA

The best pasta you will ever eat is that which you make fresh at home. Salt, oil and egg content can be controlled according to the tastes and dietary needs of those who will eat it. The results more than justify the time and effort spent to make fresh pasta.

ABOUT FLOURS

Unbleached bread flour makes a firmer pasta with more of a "bite," but all-purpose flour can be used for all of these recipes. Semolina or hard wheat durum flours can be substituted for at least part of the flour in most recipes. The best semolina flour is finely ground and is often specifically labeled as being for pasta. Pasta made with semolina flour will require extra liquid, and needs to rest longer before being rolled out. We don't recommend making dough using only semolina flour unless you have a pasta machine.

ABOUT EGGS

Always use the freshest eggs available. The eggs used in the recipes in this book are Grade A large. If using other than large eggs, mix the yolks and whites gently and use 3 tbs. of the mixture for each egg called for in the recipe. Eggs allowed to come to room temperature blend the best with flour.

BASIC HOMEMADE PASTA

This recipe makes slightly over a pound of delicious pasta.

2 cups unbleached bread flour
$1/2$ tsp. salt
3 large eggs, room temperature
2 tbs. olive oil
1–2 tbs. water if needed

MIXING PASTA DOUGH

Mixing pasta by hand: Combine flour and salt. Place in a dome on the counter or mixing surface. Make a well in flour. Break eggs into well, add olive oil, and with a kitchen fork gently beat eggs and pull a little of the flour from the edges into eggs. Continue stirring until eggs and most of the flour are combined and mixture is too stiff to continue mixing with a fork. Gently knead in remaining flour the same way you would knead bread dough; pushing, folding and turning for about 10 minutes, or until the dough is smooth and elastic. You will find that handmade pasta dough is more difficult to knead than bread dough. Wrap the dough in plastic wrap and rest at room temperature for at least 20 minutes before rolling and cutting.

Mixing pasta with a heavy duty mixer: Use any of the pasta recipes in this book. Place all ingredients in a mixer bowl. Beat with paddle or kneading hook until dough forms a ball and cleans the sides of bowl. Turn out of bowl and if dough is sticky, knead in a little more flour. Wrap dough in plastic wrap and let rest for at least 20 minutes before rolling and cutting.

Mixing pasta with a food processor: The food processor makes easy work of mixing a 1-pound recipe of pasta dough. With the metal blade in place, combine flour and salt in the workbowl and pulse a few times to mix well. Break eggs into a measuring cup, add olive oil and other ingredients and pour through the feed tube while processor is running. In about 15 to 20 seconds all ingredients will be mixed and sides of bowl will be clean. Pasta will have the texture of coarse meal, but will hold together when pinched between thumb and forefinger. It should not stick to the fingers. If pasta is dry or not completely mixed, add 1 tsp. water, process for a few seconds more, and check again. If pasta dough is sticky, add more flour 1 tbs. at a time until proper consistency is reached. Remove dough from workbowl and gather into a ball. Because the food processor has already partially kneaded the dough you will only have to knead it a minute or two until smooth. Wrap dough in plastic wrap. Let rest for at least 20 minutes before rolling out.

ROLLING PASTA DOUGH

Rolling by hand: Divide rested dough into quarters. Remove $1/4$ from plastic wrap and rewrap remaining pieces. Dust a heavy rolling pin with flour. On a lightly floured surface roll out piece of dough into a large thin rectangular shape about

$1/16$-inch thick. Repeat rolling with remaining pieces of dough. Place rolled pasta pieces on a clean towel and let rest for a few minutes until they feel dry to the touch and look slightly leathery. The pasta is now ready to cut. Drying dough before cutting will help prevent cut noodles from sticking together.

Rolling with a roller-type machine: There are two kinds of roller machines: hand-cranked and electric. Both knead and roll the pasta dough in the same way.

The advantage of the electric machine is that you have two free hands for handling dough.

After pasta dough has been mixed either by hand, with a heavy duty mixer or with a food processor as directed above, allow to rest for 20 minutes. Divide dough into 3 or 4 pieces and knead with machine instead of by hand. Set pasta machine rollers at the widest setting and run dough through machine until it becomes smooth and pliable. Fold dough into thirds lengthwise after each pass, and run through machine again. When dough is pliable and very smooth, set rollers to the next narrowest setting, fold dough in half and run through rollers two times. Set rollers to the next narrowest setting and repeat rolling and narrowing until desired thickness is reached.

CUTTING PASTA DOUGH

Cutting by hand: Roll dry, but still pliable, dough loosely into a flat roll about 3 inches wide. Cut pasta with a very sharp knife into desired widths. Press down on the knife firmly and cut without sawing. Keep slices as even as possible. As soon as the whole roll has been cut, unroll so noodles can dry further. Fettuccine is cut about $1/4$-inch wide; other noodles can range from $3/8$ inch to 1 inch; manicotti and cannelloni wrappers are made by cutting pasta in 3- or 4-inch squares. The squares are cooked and then wrapped around a filling to form a cylinder.

Cutting pasta with a hand-cranked roller machine: Allow rolled pasta dough to dry for 15 to 20 minutes before cutting. Fit the machine with desired cutting attachment. Before running dough through cutting rollers, cut sheets of pasta into strips that fit the machine and are the length you want finished pasta to be. Lightly flour dough if it is at all sticky, and run through cutter roller.

It is important that you NEVER wash your roller machine. It should be carefully cleaned with a soft brush. The dried particles will fall out easily.

Cutting pasta with an electric roller machine: This machines operates exactly as the hand-cranked machine. Follow the same directions. In addition to freeing your hands, this machine also gets the job done in a hurry. NEVER wash this machine. Brush the dried particles out with a soft brush.

DRYING PASTA

If you've just made a batch of delicious pasta, you're probably going to want to eat it as soon as possible. However, it can be made ahead of time and allowed to dry. Once pasta is thoroughly dry, it can be stored in an airtight container just as though it were a commercial product. To dry, take strands of pasta and loop them around your fingers to make little nests. Dry on a kitchen towel or cooling rack. Or, hang the long strands on a rack or over the back of a chair, or even on a clothes drying rack. Depending on humidity, it usually takes pasta about 4 to 6 hours to dry.

COOKING PASTA

Start with a large, deep kettle. For each pound of pasta bring about six quarts water to a full rolling boil. Add 2 tbs. kosher salt and pasta. Keep water boiling while pasta is cooking. It is not necessary to break long pasta, as it will soften and slide into the water (breaking pasta does make it more manageable to eat, however). Do not cover pot while cooking pasta. Do not overcook pasta. It should be firm to the bite, but not too chewy (*al dente*). Dried homemade pasta cooks in 5 to 6 minutes. Fresh homemade pasta is usually done in 2 to 3 minutes. Commercial dried pasta generally takes about 8 minutes to cook. Follow the package directions for each variety. The only sure way to tell when pasta is cooked "to the bite" or *al dente* is to periodically fish out a strand and bite it. For homemade fresh pasta, start tasting soon after the water returns to a boil. For commercial dried pasta, start tasting a minute or two before package directions say it will be done. Stir pasta with a long-handled fork or pasta fork two or three times during the cooking. Drain pasta into a large strainer, or if using a pasta pot with a strainer insert, lift strainer out of the water and let water run back into the pot. Do not rinse pasta that will be served hot. Do not allow it to become dry in the strainer, and save a few tablespoons of cooking water to add to pasta if it seems dry after it has been sauced. The best way to combine cooked pasta with sauce is to pour drained pasta into the skillet containing hot sauce and continue to cook over low heat for another minute, tossing to combine. Have a warm serving dish or plates ready. Serve immediately.

Keeping cooked pasta hot until serving: Pasta is always best when cooked, drained and sauced immediately before serving. If an unexpected delay occurs, cooked, well-drained pasta can be kept warm for no more than 30 minutes by returning it to the hot cooking pot. Toss with 2 tbs. softened butter or olive oil, cover pot and place in a "warm" 200° oven until ready to sauce and serve. Undercook pasta by a minute or two if you anticipate that serving may be delayed. Unsauced leftover pasta can be reheated by immersing briefly in boiling water immediately prior to saucing. Leftover sauced pasta reheats well in the microwave.

QUICK PASTA SAUCES

Here are some extra-quick sauces that can be made from start to finish in less time than it takes to bring the water to a boil and cook the pasta. A little melted butter and some good grated cheese on hot pasta can be just as satisfying as a more elaborate sauce with many ingredients and a long preparation time. For a perfect treat anytime, try tossing grated fontina, mozzarella, Gouda or a mild cheddar and 2 tbs. melted butter with a hot, well-drained pasta. Or toss cooked pasta with a fresh salsa, hot or mildly spiced, and top with grated cheese. Pasta pairs deliciously with a great variety of cheeses, vegetables, seafood, herbs, nuts and spices.

When making these quick sauces, assemble the ingredients first because there won't be time once you start cooking. Put the appropriate amount of water (at least six quarts for one pound of pasta) in a large pot and start it heating; then start the sauce. The amount of pasta for a serving, and how much sauce to put on it, is a matter of individual preference. In general, 12 ounces of fresh pasta, or 8 ounces of dried pasta will make 3 to 4 medium servings when cooked. Don't forget, fresh egg pastas pair well with butter and cheese, and dried pasta shapes adapt well to sauces based on olive oil.

Try some of these sauces and then make your own favorite combinations. Some great recipes can result from spur-of-the-moment inspiration.

PASTA WITH CLASSIC GARLIC AND OIL SAUCE

Preparation time: 10 minutes
Servings: 3–4

This is the simplest of all sauce preparations for any kind of pasta. Serve alone with a green salad or with roasted, broiled or barbecued meats.

12 oz. fresh pasta, or 8 oz. dried
2–3 cloves garlic, finely chopped
3 tbs. chopped fresh basil, or 1 tsp. dried
1/4 cup chopped fresh flat-leaf parsley
salt and freshly ground black pepper to taste
1/4 cup extra virgin olive oil

While pasta is cooking, chop garlic and place in a serving bowl with basil, parsley, salt and pepper; steep while pasta is cooking. Warm olive oil in a small saucepan until hot to the touch and pour over garlic mixture. Pour hot well-drained pasta into bowl and toss to combine. Season with salt and generous grinds of black pepper. Serve immediately on warm plates.

PASTA WITH BUTTER AND CHEESE SAUCE

Preparation time: 15 minutes
Servings: 3–4

With only butter and cheese in the refrigerator, you can make this delicious, satisfying sauce. Try with Basic Homemade Pasta, *page 9.*

12 oz. fresh egg noodles, or 8 oz. dried
1 stick (1/4 lb.) unsalted butter
1 tsp. dried oregano or basil
salt and freshly ground pepper to taste
1/2 cup freshly grated Parmesan cheese

While pasta is cooking, heat butter gently in a large skillet until barely melted. Add herbs, salt and pepper. Add cooked, well-drained pasta and cheese and toss quickly. If pasta appears to be dry, add 1 to 2 tbs. pasta cooking water and toss to blend. Serve immediately on warm plates.

Wine suggestion: Pinot blanc or Merlot

PASTA WITH FRESH TOMATO AND GARLIC SAUCE

Preparation time: 15 minutes
Servings: 3–4

If you have time, make this uncooked sauce an hour ahead and let stand at room temperature to allow the flavors to develop.

8 oz. dried spaghetti or tagliarini, or 12 oz. fresh
3 large ripe tomatoes, peeled, seeded and coarsely chopped
2 tbs. chopped fresh basil
1 tbs. chopped fresh chives
2 tbs. chopped fresh flat-leaf parsley or cilantro
3 cloves garlic, finely chopped
2 tbs. extra virgin olive oil
1/2 cup finely grated mozzarella or fontina cheese
salt and freshly ground black pepper to taste
freshly grated Parmesan cheese

Combine tomatoes, basil, chives, parsley, garlic, olive oil cheese, salt and pepper in a large heated serving bowl. Pour hot, well-drained pasta into bowl, add cheese and toss to combine. Serve immediately on heated plates. Pass more cheese if desired.

PASTA WITH
CLASSIC PESTO SAUCE

Preparation time: 20 minutes
Servings: 4–5

Fragrant fresh basil leaves, garlic, pine nuts or walnuts and olive oil make a delicious sauce for any shape pasta.

1 lb. fresh pasta, or 12 oz. dried
2 cups lightly packed fresh basil leaves
3 large cloves garlic
3/4 cup toasted pine nuts or chopped
   walnuts

3/4 cup extra virgin olive oil
3/4 cup freshly grated Parmesan cheese
1/2 tsp. salt, or to taste
freshly ground pepper

While pasta is cooking, place basil leaves, garlic, nuts and olive oil in a food processor workbowl or blender container. Process until ingredients are well mixed, scraping down sides of container once or twice. Process until mixture is fairly smooth. Pour into a large serving bowl and stir in cheese, salt and pepper. Pour hot, well-drained pasta into bowl and toss to combine.

Variation: Cook 1 cup orzo or other rice-shaped pasta according to package directions. Stir in 1/3 cup pesto sauce. Fill 4 hollowed-out, medium tomatoes with mixture. Top with Parmesan cheese and bake in a 375° oven for 15 minutes. Serve hot with barbecued lamb or steaks.

PASTA SALSA FRESCA

Preparation time: 15 minutes
Servings: 2–3

Take a container of your favorite fresh mild salsa from the deli case, toss it with pasta and top with avocado, cheddar cheese and black olives for a great-tasting lunch or supper. Or serve as a side dish with barbecued chicken or fish.

8 oz. dried orecchiette, radiatore or
    small shell-shaped pasta
12 oz. fresh mild tomato salsa
1 avocado, peeled and diced
1/2 cup (2 oz.) coarsely grated cheddar
    cheese

1/4 cup sliced black olives, drained
salt and freshly ground pepper to taste
fresh cilantro for garnish
grated Parmesan cheese, optional

Cook pasta according to package directions. Remove lid from salsa container and heat in a microwave for about 45 seconds just to warm salsa, or heat slightly in a small saucepan. Pour hot, well-drained pasta into a warm serving bowl and toss with salsa. Add avocado pieces, cheddar cheese, olives, salt and pepper, and toss again. Top with fresh cilantro leaves and serve. Pass some grated cheese, if desired.

ANGEL HAIR PASTA WITH BLACK OLIVE PASTE

Preparation time: 15 minutes
Servings: 2

This pasta can be made while the pasta water is brought to a boil and the angel hair pasta is cooked. Double the recipe for each two people you want to serve. The robust olive paste flavors are a wonderful match for the delicate strands of angel hair pasta. Use the best Parmigiano Reggiano cheese you can buy; it does make a difference. Take this on a picnic or to a barbecue — it is delicious at room temperature.

4 oz. dried angel hair pasta
2 tbs. black olive paste or tapenade
3 tbs. half-and-half
1/4 tsp. red pepper flakes

freshly ground black pepper to taste
1 large tomato, peeled, seeded and chopped
grated Parmesan cheese for garnish

Bring pasta water to a boil. Cook pasta according to package instructions. In a warm serving bowl, combine olive paste with half-and-half. Stir in red pepper flakes and freshly ground black pepper. Drain and add hot pasta to serving bowl. Toss with other ingredients and top each serving with fresh tomato pieces. Pass Parmesan cheese.

PASTA WITH SUN-DRIED TOMATOES AND GARLIC

Preparation time: 20 minutes
Servings: 2

Use oil-packed sun-dried tomatoes and include a little of the oil for a full-flavored fast pasta dinner. Angel hair pasta cooks very quickly, so start testing it after it has cooked for 2 minutes. This recipe can be easily doubled.

4 oz. dried angel hair or capellini-shaped pasta
2 tbs. extra virgin olive oil
2 large cloves garlic, minced
2–3 tbs. slivered sun-dried tomatoes, with a little of their oil
salt to taste
generous amounts freshly ground black pepper
$1/3$ cup grated Parmesan cheese

Bring pasta water to a boil and cook pasta. In a nonstick medium skillet, add olive oil, garlic and sun-dried tomato oil, and sauté garlic for 1 to 2 minutes. Pour hot, well-drained pasta into skillet; add sun-dried tomatoes, salt, black pepper and Parmesan cheese. Toss to combine. Serve immediately on warmed plates. Pass additional Parmesan cheese.

PASTA WITH
PIQUANT PARSLEY SAUCE

Preparation time: 15 minutes
Makes: 2/3 cup

This zesty, vibrant no-cook green sauce is terrific on almost any shape of pasta. Pair it with cheese or chicken tortellini, or use it for a dressing on a cold chicken salad. If you have time, let stand for an hour before using.

2 cloves garlic
leaves from 1 bunch flat-leaf parsley
    (about 2 cups, loosely packed)
2 anchovies, drained
2 tbs. capers, drained
1/3 cup extra virgin olive oil

1 tsp. Dijon mustard
2 tbs. ricotta cheese
1 tbs. lemon juice
freshly ground pepper to taste
12 oz. fresh pasta, or 8 oz. dried
grated Parmesan cheese for garnish

Using a food processor, with the motor running, drop garlic into feed tube and process until chopped. Add parsley leaves and process until well chopped. Add anchovies, capers, oil, mustard, ricotta, lemon juice and pepper. Process until well combined but not smooth. Pour into a large serving bowl, cover and let stand for about 1 hour before using.

Cook pasta according to package directions. Pour hot, well-drained pasta into sauce and toss to mix well. Pass grated Parmesan cheese.

Variation: Add slivers of prosciutto or cooked ham to the pasta before tossing.

PASTA WITH GOAT CHEESE AND CHERRY TOMATOES

Preparation time: 15 minutes
Servings: 2

Creamy goat cheese melts into thin strands of angel hair pasta and is accented with cherry tomatoes and basil. If available, use a combination of orange, yellow and red cherry tomatoes to make a particularly colorful dish. Double the recipe for more servings.

4 oz. dried angel hair or capellini pasta, or 6 oz. fresh
1 tbs. extra virgin olive oil
4 oz. creamy fresh goat cheese, crumbled
2 cups small cherry tomatoes, stemmed, cut in half, seeded
1 pinch hot pepper flakes
salt and freshly ground pepper to taste
20 fresh basil leaves, cut into ribbons

Heat pasta water and cook pasta. Place olive oil and goat cheese in a large warm serving bowl. Pour hot, well-drained pasta into serving bowl and toss to melt cheese. Add tomatoes, pepper flakes, salt, pepper and basil. Toss again and serve on warm plates.

PASTA WITH ZESTY TOMATO AND HOT PEPPER SAUCE

Preparation time: 15 minutes
Servings: 3–4

For the very best flavor, use perfectly ripe Romano or plum tomatoes if they are available. Small perfectly ripe regular tomatoes are almost as good.

8 oz. dried fettuccine or tagliarini noodles, or 12 oz. fresh
1/4 cup extra virgin olive oil
6–8 Romano tomatoes, about 1 1/4 lb., peeled, cut
   into quarters and seeded
1 large clove garlic, finely chopped
2 tsp. fresh oregano, or 1/2 tsp. dried
1–2 small fresh hot peppers, stemmed, seeded and
   finely chopped
salt and freshly ground black pepper to taste
freshly grated Parmesan cheese

While pasta is cooking, heat olive oil in a large skillet. Add tomatoes, garlic, oregano, hot peppers, salt and pepper. Sauté over medium heat for 4 to 5 minutes, or until tomatoes have softened but still hold their shape. Pour hot, well-drained pasta into skillet and toss to combine. Serve immediately on warm plates. Pass Parmesan cheese.

PASTA WITH SPICY PEPPERONI AND MUSHROOM SAUCE

Preparation time: 15 minutes
Servings: 3–4

This hearty sauce is perfect when you're hungry, but short on time.

12 oz. fresh pasta, or 8 oz. dried
1 tbs. extra virgin olive oil
1/4 lb. pepperoni, skin removed and
  thinly sliced
1/2 lb. fresh mushrooms, thinly sliced
4–5 green onions, including 1 inch
  green part, cut into 1/4-inch slices

1/2 cup heavy cream
salt and freshly ground pepper to taste
chopped fresh flat-leaf parsley for
  garnish
freshly grated Pecorino or Asiago
  cheese

While pasta is cooking, heat oil in a large skillet. Sauté pepperoni for 3 to 4 minutes. Remove pepperoni with a slotted spoon and set aside. Add sliced mushrooms and onions to skillet. Sauté for 4 to 5 minutes over medium heat, until mushrooms are soft. Add cream, pepperoni, salt and pepper and heat through. Pour hot, well-drained pasta into skillet and toss to combine. Garnish with parsley. Serve immediately on warm plates. Pass cheese.

Wine suggestion: Barbera or full-bodied Zinfandel

PASTA WITH TUNA, CHERRY TOMATOES AND OLIVE SAUCE

Preparation time: 15 minutes
Servings: 4

Use oil-packed tuna for this easy Mediterranean-style sauce.

8 oz. dried fusilli or other pasta
1 can (6½ oz.) oil-packed tuna
1 tbs. tapenade or black olive paste
2 cups cherry tomatoes, stemmed, cut into halves or quarters if large
3 tbs. rinsed, drained small capers
½ cup lightly packed fresh basil leaves, cut into ribbons
½ cup finely diced fresh mozzarella cheese
salt and generous amounts freshly ground black pepper

While pasta is cooking, place tuna with its oil in a large serving bowl. Add tapenade, cherry tomatoes, capers and basil. Stir to combine. Add hot, drained pasta to bowl, distribute mozzarella cheese over pasta and toss to combine. Adjust seasoning with salt and pepper. Serve immediately on warm plates.

Note: If using water-packed tuna, drain well and add 2 tbs. extra virgin olive oil.

PASTA WITH ROASTED CORN, TOMATO AND BASIL SAUCE

Preparation time: 30 minutes
Servings: 3–4

Use your best olive oil in this tomato and basil sauce.

8 oz. dried bowtie pasta (farfalle)
4 ears fresh sweet corn
2 tbs. extra virgin olive oil
salt and freshly ground pepper to taste
3 large ripe tomatoes, peeled, seeded and chopped
3–4 tbs. extra virgin olive oil

2 small jalapeño chile peppers, stemmed, seeded and finely chopped
1 cup lightly packed fresh basil leaves, cut into ribbons
salt and freshly ground black pepper
freshly grated Parmesan or dry Monterey Jack cheese for garnish

Heat oven to 400°. Line a jelly roll pan or rimmed baking sheet with aluminum foil. With a sharp knife, cut corn kernels from cob and place in a small bowl. Add 2 tbs. olive oil, salt and pepper. Mix well. Spread corn in a single layer on prepared baking sheet and bake for 15 to 17 minutes, until lightly browned. Stir once or twice during cooking. Remove from oven and pour into a large serving bowl. Use immediately or refrigerate until needed for pasta. Add remaining ingredients, except for cheese, to serving bowl and mix well. Add hot, well-drained pasta and mix well. Pass cheese at the table.

FETTUCCINE ALFREDO

Preparation time: 15 minutes
Servings: 3–4

This classic sauce which originated in Venice has become a restaurant favorite. It can be quickly put together and makes an elegant first course for a meal with company.

8 oz. dried fettuccine noodles, or 12 oz. fresh
2 tbs. butter
$3/4$ cup heavy cream
$1/2$ cup grated Parmesan cheese
freshly grated nutmeg
salt and freshly ground black pepper to taste

While pasta is cooking, melt butter in a large skillet. Add cream and $1/2$ of the cheese. Simmer over very low heat for 4 to 5 minutes, until sauce starts to thicken. Add hot, well-drained pasta to skillet. Lift pasta and stir to combine and coat strands. Add remaining cheese, nutmeg, salt and a generous grinding of black pepper. Serve immediately on warm plates.

Variation: Add $1/4$ tsp. hot pepper flakes to skillet when butter has melted.

SPAGHETTI CARBONARA

Preparation time: 15 minutes
Servings: 3–4

Here is a classic sauce made with bacon, eggs and cream. The Italian rolled bacon called pancetta will add special character and flavor to this dish.

12 oz. dried spaghetti, or 1 lb. fresh
1/2 lb. pancetta or bacon, thinly sliced
1 large onion, chopped
1/2 cup finely chopped fresh flat-leaf
  parsley

2 large eggs, room temperature
3/4 cup freshly grated Parmesan cheese
1/4 tsp. hot pepper flakes, optional
1/2 cup heavy cream

Begin heating pasta water so it will be ready when needed. Cut pancetta or bacon into 1-inch pieces. Sauté in a large skillet until crisp. Remove bacon pieces. Pour off all but 2 tbs. fat. Sauté onion in bacon fat for 3 to 4 minutes, until soft. Return bacon to skillet. In a small bowl, combine parsley, eggs, Parmesan cheese, pepper flakes and cream and blend with a fork. Cook pasta and pour hot, well-drained pasta into skillet. Quickly pour egg mixture over hot pasta and mix well. Serve immediately on warm plates.

Wine suggestion: a light, fruity Zinfandel or Merlot

"REFRIGERATOR" PASTA

One evening we jokingly told friends that we had refrigerator pasta for dinner. When asked for an explanation, we gave a sketch for a very quick and easy main dish using available ingredients from the refrigerator. It is more of an outline than a real recipe. There are a few ingredients that you should always have on hand:

heavy cream (ultra-pasteurized kind will keep for weeks)
good grating cheese
sweet cream butter
fresh garlic

extra virgin olive oil
tomato paste in a tube
red pepper flakes
yellow or green onions
fresh flat-leaf parsley

These ingredients by themselves can be used to make three or four great pasta sauces in the time it takes to boil the pasta water. After you have a base, rummage in the refrigerator and see what else you can find. Look for:

mushrooms
red, yellow or green bell peppers
ripe tomatoes
leftover vegetables, or easily defrosted frozen vegetables such as peas

leftover chicken, turkey or ham
tubes of sun-dried tomato, black olive or anchovy paste
soft cheese that can be cubed and added to the pasta to melt

If the refrigerator is bare, look in the cupboard for:

canned chopped clams

canned shrimp, crab or anchovies

canned tuna or salmon

canned mushrooms

canned pimientos or green chiles

olives, olive paste, or tapenade

canned chicken stock or beef broth

Put water on to boil. Based on available ingredients, decide on which pasta shape to cook. Decide whether you will have a cream- or oil-based sauce. Put butter or oil (about 1 tbs. per serving of pasta) in a large skillet and heat on medium. Add a few red pepper flakes and onion or garlic and sauté over medium heat until flavor is released. When water boils, add a generous quantity of coarse salt and then pasta. Stir pasta once or twice to make sure it doesn't stick together.

Add any ingredients to skillet that need to be sautéed or cooked. Just before pasta is done, add cream and remaining ingredients and heat through. Pour hot, well-drained pasta into skillet. Toss and stir to combine pasta with sauce. Add freshly grated cheese and black pepper if desired. Toss one more time and serve immediately on heated plates. Sprinkle with chopped parsley and some chopped fresh tomato. Pass more cheese at the table.

PASTA SOUPS

Pasta is a natural for soups. The Italians have a myriad of soup recipes using pasta with beans, tomatoes and vegetables to make hearty, satisfying soups. Asian cuisines, too, feature pasta in the form of fresh and dried noodles. Their dishes incorporate noodles, bits of vegetables and chicken or seafood into a great variety of soups that are often eaten as snacks, or even for breakfast. Ramen has become an international favorite, and is unexcelled for convenience, ease of preparation and low cost.

These pasta soups range from light to hearty. Cold *Lemon Pasta Soup* and *Green Chile Pasta Soup* make delicious starters for a dinner. *Pasta Bean Soup* is a filling, hearty winter entrée. *Pasta in Broth* gives directions for making a flavorful soup base using canned broth. We prefer low sodium broths and stocks. Salt can always be added to soup if needed.

PASTA IN BROTH

If you don't have homemade broth available, here is a delicious substitute. Just add pasta and you have a light soup. We prefer low sodium broth.

2 cans (14½ oz. each) beef or chicken broth (or one of each)
½ cup finely chopped onion
½ cup finely chopped carrot
1 bay leaf

¼ cup finely chopped celery, including some leaves
2–3 whole black peppercorns
2 oz. dried thin pasta (orzo, shells or other small pasta)

Combine broth, onion, carrot, seasonings and celery in a medium saucepan. Bring to a boil and simmer gently, uncovered, for 20 minutes. Strain through a sieve or damp cheesecloth, pressing as much juice as possible out of vegetables. Discard vegetables. Measure stock. If necessary, add enough water to bring stock up to 4 cups. Return liquid to saucepan and bring to a boil. Add thin pasta broken into 1-inch pieces, or orzo, alphabets or other small pasta. Cook until pasta is done. Serve immediately in warm bowls.

The broth will keep in the refrigerator for 2 to 3 days. If you are going to keep it longer, bring to a full boil, cool and return to the refrigerator, or freeze.

LEMON PASTA SOUP

Preparation time: 15 minutes
Servings: 6

This soup can be served hot or cold, but it is particularly nice chilled and served in pretty glass bowls. Garnish with thin lemon slices.

$1/2$ cup tiny pasta shapes (stars, shells or orzo)

6 cups chicken broth

$1/8$ tsp. white pepper

salt to taste

3 large eggs

$1/3$ cup lemon juice

1 lemon, thinly sliced, for garnish

Combine pasta, chicken broth and pepper in a saucepan. Bring to a boil. Cover and simmer until pasta is tender, about 10 minutes. Remove from heat and season to taste with salt. Whisk eggs in a separate bowl until pale yellow. Slowly add lemon juice to eggs. Carefully stir some of the hot broth into egg-lemon mixture, beating continuously. Add tempered egg-lemon mixture to remaining hot broth. If serving hot, ladle into hot soup cups and garnish with lemon.To serve cold, cool soup, cover and refrigerate for 3 to 4 hours or overnight. Serve very cold and stir well before ladling into serving bowls. Garnish each serving with one or two thin lemon slices.

Note: Different brands of canned chicken broth vary in saltiness, so taste carefully before adding additional salt.

GLORIFIED RAMEN NOODLE SOUP

Preparation time: 15 minutes
Servings: 2–3

Ramen is easy and nutritious. Discard the sodium-laden flavor packets and use your own broth.

2 cans (14½ oz. each) low-sodium
   chicken or beef broth
1 cup water
2 pkg. (3 oz. each) ramen noodles
½ tsp. toasted sesame oil
1 tbs. soy sauce
white pepper

½ cup frozen peas, defrosted
3 green onions, including 1 inch green
   part, thinly sliced
½ cup finely diced cooked ham,
   chicken, pork or shrimp, optional
fresh cilantro leaves for garnish

Heat chicken or beef broth and water in a medium saucepan. Discard ramen seasoning packets and break noodles into several pieces to make soup easier to eat. Add remaining ingredients, return to a boil and simmer for 5 minutes. Serve immediately in warm bowls. Garnish with cilantro leaves.

Variation: Substitute 1 cup coarsely chopped fresh spinach leaves for peas. Cook until leaves wilt.

PASTA AND BEAN SOUP

Preparation time: 30 minutes
Servings: 4–5

This hearty nutritious soup is especially good in cold weather. Add a green salad and some garlic bread to make a satisfying meal.

2 tbs. olive oil
1 small onion, diced
1 stalk celery, diced
1 large carrot, diced
1 large can (49½ oz.) chicken broth
3 tbs. tomato paste

4 oz. dried pasta (shells or macaroni)
2 cans (15½ oz. each) cannellini beans
   with liquid
chopped fresh flat-leaf parsley for
   garnish
grated Parmesan cheese for garnish

Heat olive oil in a large saucepan. Add onion, celery and carrot and cook over low heat for 3 to 4 minutes, until vegetables have softened, but not browned.

Add chicken broth and tomato paste and simmer over medium-high heat for 15 minutes. Add pasta and simmer until almost cooked. Puree 1 can of the beans in a food processor or blender until smooth and add to saucepan.

Add second can of beans and continue cooking until pasta is tender. Taste carefully for salt and add generous grinds of black pepper. Serve immediately. Garnish with parsley and pass Parmesan cheese.

GREEN CHILE PASTA SOUP

Preparation time: 30 minutes
Servings: 3–4

Creamy and mildly spicy, this makes a delicious winter soup.

1 tbs. butter
6 green onions, including 1 inch green part, thinly sliced
1 can (4 oz.) canned whole green chiles, or to taste
1 can (14½ oz.) chicken broth
3 oz. thin dried pasta or small shells

½ tsp. cumin
salt
¼ tsp. white pepper
1 cup half-and-half
fresh cilantro leaves or diced pimiento for garnish

Heat butter in a small skillet. Sauté onions until soft. Drain green chiles, remove stem and seeds. Place chiles, onion and a little of the chicken broth in a food processor or blender bowl and process until mixture is smooth. Cook pasta according to package directions. (If using thin pasta, break in 1-inch pieces.) Drain. Bring chicken broth to a boil in a medium saucepan. Add chile mixture, cumin, salt, pepper and cooked pasta. Add half-and-half and heat through. Pour into warm soup bowls and garnish with cilantro or pimiento. Serve immediately.

INNOVATIVE PASTA SALADS

Pasta salads make splendid side dishes to go with chicken, fish, ham or other meat entrées. They can also be the featured dish for luncheons, picnics and cold suppers.

The only time hot cooked pasta is drained and rinsed with cold water is when it is going to be used in a salad. This step cools the pasta before it is combined with the dressing and other ingredients. It is also important to toss drained pasta immediately with 1 tbs. oil or some of the dressing to keep it from sticking together.

Tender, delicately flavored pasta complements the crisp, colorful vegetable pieces and slivers of meat that are often used in salads. The most piquant dressings are quickly absorbed and become wonderfully mellow as they chill. Remember to prepare most pasta salads 1 to 2 hours ahead so they can chill and allow flavors time to harmonize. Stir the salads after an hour or so of chilling. If they appear dry, add a little more mayonnaise or oil to moisten. Salads should be removed from the refrigerator 15 to 20 minutes before serving so they are not icy cold. Garnish with parsley, cilantro or other toppings just before serving. If salads are to be served outside, it is important to keep them as cold as possible and out of the sun to avoid spoilage.

ASPARAGUS AND ORANGE PASTA SALAD

Preparation time: 30 minutes
Refrigerate: 1–2 hours
Servings: 3–4

This salad captures the essence of spring, featuring delicious young asparagus and orange segments tossed with pasta. Orange zest adds interest to the creamy dressing.

16 thin spears fresh asparagus
1 tbs. extra virgin olive oil
1 medium leek, white part only
2 cloves garlic, minced
1 tbs. grated fresh ginger
1 dash red pepper flakes
$1/2$ cup mayonnaise
grated zest and segments of 2 small oranges
8 oz. dried pasta shapes (gemellini or corkscrew)
salt and white pepper

Bring pasta water to a boil. Cut asparagus spears into ½-inch diagonal slices. Cut leek into strips ¼-inch wide by 2 inches long. Place in a sieve and rinse well to remove any sand. Heat olive oil in a small nonstick skillet. Sauté leeks, ginger, garlic and red pepper flakes over low heat for about 10 minutes, until leeks are soft but not brown.

Place mayonnaise in a small bowl. Using a fine grater, grate zest from both oranges. Stir zest into mayonnaise. Carefully cut remaining rind and membrane from oranges and segment oranges. Squeeze any remaining juice from membrane into mayonnaise. Set aside.

Cook pasta according to package directions. About 2 minutes before pasta is done, add asparagus pieces. When pasta is cooked, drain well and rinse with cold water. Toss pasta and asparagus in a large bowl with leek and garlic mixture. When cool to the touch, add mayonnaise and orange segments. Toss to combine. Chill for 1 to 2 hours before serving.

BANGKOK NOODLE SALAD

Preparation time: 30 minutes
Refrigerate: 1 hour
Servings: 3–4

Chunky peanut butter dressing, slivered cucumber, chicken, carrots and thin pasta strands topped with crunchy chopped peanuts make a great lunch or picnic salad. Wait 1 hour before serving for flavors to combine. This is best made and eaten the same day.

4 oz. dried thin pasta (capellini) or 6 oz. fresh
4 green onions, including 1 inch green part, thinly sliced
1/2 cup coarsely grated or thinly sliced carrot
1/2 cup thin strips peeled cucumber
1 cup thin strips cooked chicken
1/2 cup fresh cilantro leaves for garnish
1/2 cup chopped unsalted dry-roasted peanuts for garnish

DRESSING

1/4 cup chunky peanut butter
2 tbs. soy sauce
1 tsp. Dijon mustard

1/4 tsp. red pepper flakes
2 tbs. rice wine vinegar
2 tsp. sesame oil

Combine in a small bowl and stir until thick and creamy.

Break pasta strands in half and cook pasta according to package directions. Rinse with cold water and drain well. Pour into a large bowl and immediately toss with dressing. Add carrots, cucumber and chicken strips. Toss to combine.

Refrigerate for 1 hour before serving. Garnish with fresh cilantro and chopped peanuts.

CELERY ROOT AND PASTA SALAD

Preparation time: 30 minutes
Servings: 3–4
Refrigerate: 2 hours

Use spinach pasta for a pretty contrast with the white celery root and carrot strips. Add strips of prosciutto or salami for variation. The best celery roots are about 4 inches in diameter. The larger ones sometimes have soft centers.

4 oz. dried spinach linguine
2 tbs. Dijon mustard
3 tbs. rice wine vinegar
1/3 cup extra virgin olive oil
salt and freshly ground pepper
1 cup thin strips peeled celery root
1 large or 2 small carrots, cut into 3-inch by 1/4-inch strips
4 oz. provolone or smoked Gouda cheese, cut into thin strips
1/4 cup finely chopped fresh flat-leaf parsley

Bring pasta water to a boil. Break linguine strands into thirds and cook. About 2 minutes before pasta is done, add carrot strips to pot. Make dressing by whisking together mustard and vinegar in a large bowl. Slowly add oil and continue to whisk until mixture thickens. Season with salt and pepper.

Peel celery root. Cut into thin slices and then into strips, or use the julienne blade in your food processor. The celery root should be added to the dressing as soon as possible so it does not turn brown.

Immediately combine hot, well-drained pasta and carrots with dressing. Add celery root mixture. When cool to the touch add cheese strips and parsley. Toss to combine. This can be refrigerated for 2 hours before serving.

GARDEN VEGETABLE PASTA SALAD

Preparation time: 30 minutes
Servings: 4
Refrigerate: 1–2 hours

Crisp fresh vegetable pieces accent radiatore, gemellini, fusilli or the pasta shape of your choice. Garnish with fresh basil just before serving. Add a cup of diced cooked chicken, ham or salad shrimp for a nice variation.

8 oz. dried pasta (radiatore, gemellini or fusilli)
¼ cup extra virgin olive oil, divided
¼ cup red onion, finely chopped
½ medium red, yellow or green bell pepper, diced
1 tender stalk celery, diced
1 small carrot, coarsely grated
1 medium tomato, peeled, seeded and chopped

1 dash red pepper flakes
2 tsp. Dijon mustard
3 tbs. extra virgin olive oil
1 tbs. rice wine vinegar
1 tsp. lemon juice
salt and freshly ground pepper
¼ cup grated Parmesan cheese
¼ cup thinly sliced fresh basil

Bring pasta water to a boil and cook pasta. Immediately rinse with cold water, drain and toss in a large bowl with 1 tbs. olive oil. Add onion, pepper, celery, carrot, tomato and red pepper flakes.

In a small bowl, whisk together Dijon mustard, remaining olive oil, rice wine vinegar, lemon juice, salt and pepper. When mixture forms an emulsion, add to pasta and vegetables. Add ½ of the cheese and toss to combine. Pour into a serving bowl and top with remaining Parmesan cheese and basil. This salad can be served immediately or refrigerated for 1 to 2 hours before serving.

DELI PASTA SALAD

Preparation time: 30 minutes
Refrigerate: 2 hours
Servings: 4–6

This hearty salad is easily assembled from ingredients purchased at the deli.

8 oz. dried egg noodles
1 tbs. extra virgin olive oil
3 oz. mortadella, bologna or ham, thinly sliced
3 oz. Gruyère or Swiss cheese, thinly sliced
1 large German-style pickle or dill pickle

1 large or 2 small tart apples, peeled and cored
1 1/2 tbs. Worcestershire sauce
3–4 tbs. mayonnaise
1/2 tsp. white pepper
2 tbs. freshly grated Parmesan cheese
2 tbs. minced fresh flat-leaf parsley for garnish

Cook noodles. Rinse with cold water and drain well. Place in a large bowl and immediately toss noodles with olive oil. Cut meats, cheese and pickle into strips about the same width and thickness as the noodles. Coarsely grate apple. Combine noodles with meats, cheese, apple and pickle. In a small bowl, combine Worcestershire sauce, mayonnaise, white pepper and grated cheese. Add to pasta. Gently toss with two forks until well mixed. Refrigerate for at least 2 hours before serving. Just before serving garnish with parsley.

MACARONI SALAD

Preparation time: 30 minutes
Refrigerate: 1–2 hours
Servings: 4–6

This is a perfect picnic salad. For even better flavor, make it a few hours ahead and let it mellow in the refrigerator until serving.

1 cup uncooked salad macaroni
2 hard-cooked eggs, chopped
1 tbs. minced green onion
1/4 cup minced sweet pickle
1/4 cup finely diced celery
1 tbs. capers, rinsed and drained
1 cup cooked green peas
2 tbs. chopped pimiento

1/2 cup mayonnaise
2 tbs. pickle juice
1 tsp. prepared mustard
1/4 tsp. white pepper
1 tsp. salt
2 tbs. sour cream
2 tbs. minced fresh flat-leaf parsley

Cook macaroni in boiling water according to package directions. Immediately rinse with cold water and drain well. Place in a large bowl. Add eggs, onion, pickle, celery, capers, peas and pimiento. In a small bowl, combine mayonnaise, pickle juice, mustard, pepper, salt and sour cream and mix well. Add to macaroni mixture with parsley. Toss lightly with two forks to combine. Refrigerate for 1 to 2 hours before serving.

PATIO SHELL SALAD

Preparation time: 30 minutes
Refrigerate: 2 hours
Servings: 6 to 8

This hearty salad features red kidney beans, yellow corn, green chiles and cumin for a Southwestern flavor. Serve with grilled meat.

4 oz. dried small pasta shells
1 can (15½ oz.) red kidney beans, well drained
1 can (12 oz.) whole kernel corn, well drained
4–5 green onions, including 1 inch green part, finely chopped
4–5 tbs. finely chopped canned green chiles

½ tsp. ground cumin
1 tsp. dried oregano
1 tbs. lemon juice
½ cup mayonnaise
½ tsp. salt, or to taste
½ tsp. freshly ground black pepper

Cook pasta according to package directions. Immediately rinse with cold water and drain well. Rinse kidney beans under cold water and drain well. Rinse corn and drain. Combine pasta, beans, corn and remaining ingredients. Gently toss with two forks. Add a little more mayonnaise if pasta seems dry.

Chill in refrigerator for at least 2 hours before serving.

PASTA-STUFFED TOMATOES

Preparation time: 30 minutes
Servings: 4

For this dish, large tomatoes are filled with a savory cooked pasta and baked to make a delicious lunch or side dish. This recipe can be easily doubled.

4 large ripe tomatoes
1 cup small dried pasta shells or salad macaroni, about 3 oz.
1 tbs. extra virgin olive oil
1 tbs. black olive paste

1 tsp. tomato paste
$1/2$ cup grated pecorino or Parmesan cheese
2 tbs. chopped fresh flat-leaf parsley
salt and freshly ground pepper to taste

Heat oven to 425.° Core tomatoes and cut a $1/2$-inch slice from each top. With a sharp spoon, remove pulp and seeds. Reserve pulp and chop into small pieces, discarding any hard cores. Sprinkle tomato shells with salt and turn upside down on paper towels to drain. Cook pasta according to package directions. Drain pasta, place in a medium bowl and toss immediately with olive oil. Add reserved tomato pulp and remaining ingredients to pasta, reserving 2 tbs. of the cheese to sprinkle over stuffed tomatoes. Mix well. Spoon pasta mixture into drained tomato shells, without packing. Sprinkle with remaining cheese. Place in a shallow baking dish, add about $1/2$ inch of water to bottom of dish and bake for 15 minutes or until tomatoes shells are hot but not collapsing. Serve hot or warm.

SESAME NOODLE SALAD

Preparation time: 30 minutes
Servings: 3–4

The fresh thin Chinese or Hong Kong style noodles used in this dish can often be found in the supermarket produce or dairy section. If you cut the noodle package in half before cooking, the noodles will be a more manageable length. Substitute fresh or dried capellini if Chinese noodles aren't available.

8 oz. fresh Chinese style noodles, or 6 oz. dried pasta
1 tbs. sesame oil
2 tbs. rice wine vinegar
1 tbs. vegetable oil
2 tbs. soy sauce
2 cloves garlic, minced
1/4 tsp. red pepper flakes
2 green onions, thinly sliced
2 oz. fresh snow peas, blanched, cut into thin strips
1 large carrot, coarsely grated
1/2 cup firm tofu, cut into thin strips, optional
1 tbs. toasted sesame seeds
fresh cilantro leaves for garnish

Cook noodles as directed on package, about 2 to 3 minutes for fresh noodles. Drain and rinse with cold water. Drain again and place in a large bowl. Toss immediately with 1 tbs. sesame oil to keep noodles from sticking together. Combine wine vinegar, vegetable oil, soy sauce, garlic and red pepper flakes in a small microwaveable bowl. Heat on high, uncovered for 30 seconds, or bring to a boil in a small saucepan and cook for 1 minute.

Combine hot wine vinegar mixture with cooked noodles, toss and add onions, snow peas and shredded carrot. If not serving immediately, refrigerate. Just before serving, toss with toasted sesame seeds and top with tofu strips and fresh cilantro leaves.

Variation: Substitute $1/2$ cup small cooked shrimp and 1 cup finely diced celery for tofu. Or substitute 1 cup finely shredded red cabbage for tofu.

SOUTH OF THE BORDER COUSCOUS SALAD

Preparation time: 30 minutes
Servings: 3–4

This light salad, full of zesty flavors of cumin, chili powder and peppers, is garnished with tomato and avocado. This salad is best made and served the same day. Serve with crisp tortilla chips.

³/₄ cup water
2 tbs. vegetable oil, divided
¹/₂ cup quick-cooking couscous
3–4 green onions, including 1 inch green part, thinly sliced
¹/₂ cup diced red or green bell peppers
1 clove garlic
¹/₄ tsp. chili powder
1 tsp. ground cumin

¹/₂ tsp. dried oregano
1 small jalapeño pepper, stemmed, minced, or to taste
¹/₂ cup peeled, finely diced jicama
1 ripe avocado, peeled and diced
1 large, ripe tomato, peeled, seeded and chopped
2 tsp. lime juice
¹/₄ cup fresh cilantro leaves for garnish

Bring water and 1 tbs. of the oil to a boil in a medium saucepan or skillet. Pour in couscous, stir, remove from heat, cover and let stand for 5 minutes. Fluff couscous with a fork and pour into a bowl so mixture can cool before adding remaining ingredients.

Heat remaining tbs. oil in a nonstick skillet. Over low heat, sauté green onions and peppers for 5 to 6 minutes. Add garlic, chili powder, cumin, oregano and jalapeño pepper. Cook for 1 to 2 minutes and add to couscous mixture.

Stir jicama, avocado, tomato and lime juice into couscous mixture. Top with fresh cilantro leaves and serve. If making ahead, stir in avocado and garnish with cilantro just before serving. Refrigerate for 1 to 2 hours before serving, if desired.

TORTELLINI AND ARTICHOKE SALAD

Preparation time: 20 minutes
Servings: 3–4

Here is a fast appetizer or luncheon salad using deli ingredients.

1 pkg. (10 oz.) fresh cheese or chicken tortellini
3–4 marinated artichoke hearts or bottoms
2–3 tbs. diced roasted red peppers or pimiento
1/4 cup mayonnaise

2 tsp. Dijon mustard
1 tbs. grated Parmesan cheese
salt to taste
white pepper
2 tbs. finely sliced fresh basil, or 1/2 tsp. dried
2 tbs. chopped fresh flat-leaf parsley

Cook tortellini as directed on package. Rinse with cold water and drain well. Toss with 1 tbs. marinated artichoke liquid to prevent sticking. Allow tortellini to cool while preparing remaining ingredients. Drain artichokes. Cut artichoke bottoms into 1/4-inch slivers. If using artichoke hearts, cut into small pieces. Combine cooled tortellini, artichokes and red peppers with mayonnaise, mustard, salt and pepper. Refrigerate if not serving immediately. Garnish with fresh basil and parsley just before serving.

Variation: Add 1/2 cup small, cooked shrimp or thin strips of prosciutto or salami.

PASTA WITH FRESH VEGETABLES

Vegetables with pasta make an attractive combination that offers a delicious contrast of textures and is very pleasing to the eye. Red, yellow and green bell peppers, orange carrots, yellow and green squash, red tomatoes, green asparagus, snow peas and tiny peas instantly provide colorful accents for the pale pasta. The vegetables in pasta dishes can be slightly cooked to provide a crunchy texture or cooked longer, their flavors releasing to add complexity to the sauce.

A quick trick for cooking vegetables is to add the prepared vegetables to the hot pasta water for the last few minutes before pasta is cooked. Drain the pasta and vegetables together and add them to the sauce.

We like to peel and seed fresh tomatoes. We peel peppers with a vegetable peeler to preserve the crispness of the raw peppers, make them easier to digest, and because it is quicker than the usual method of blistering the skin over flame and then peeling. But peeling vegetables is a personal preference. Your cooking pleasure should not be diminished by too many rules or special techniques.

Use the freshest vegetables in season and your own favorites to create delicious new variations.

FETTUCCINE WITH BROCCOLI AND CARROTS

Preparation time: 30 minutes
Servings: 3–4

Crisp vegetables add interest to this quick and colorful pasta dish. Try it with zucchini instead of broccoli.

4 medium carrots
3 cups broccoli pieces
4–5 slices pancetta or bacon, optional
8 oz. dried fettuccine noodles
2 tbs. extra virgin olive oil

5–6 green onions, including 1 inch green part, thinly sliced
2 large cloves garlic, minced
1 tbs. red wine vinegar
grated Parmesan cheese for garnish

Heat pasta water in a large pot. Cut carrots into matchsticks about 1½ inches long. Cut broccoli florets from stems, peel stems and cut into paper-thin slices. Sauté pancetta in a large skillet until crisp. Remove from skillet and crumble into small pieces. Pour out all but 2 tbs. of the pan drippings.

Begin cooking pasta now. Add olive oil to bacon drippings over medium heat. When oil is hot, add carrots, broccoli, onions and garlic. Toss to coat vegetables with oil. Cover and cook for 1 to 2 minutes. Add vinegar and cook for 1 minute. Pour hot, well-drained pasta into skillet and toss to combine. Serve immediately on warm plates. Pass Parmesan cheese.

FETTUCCINE WITH CABBAGE AND PANCETTA

Preparation time: 30 minutes
Servings: 3–4

Golden cabbage, garlic and pancetta pair well with fettuccine, linguine or egg noodles. Crisp toasted bread crumbs add a nice texture contrast. Substitute bacon if pancetta isn't available.

12 oz. dried fettuccine noodles
1/4 cup extra virgin olive oil, divided
1 cup coarsely grated fresh bread crumbs
salt and freshly ground pepper for seasoning
6 oz. thinly sliced pancetta, cut into thin ribbons
6 cups white cabbage, cored, cut into 1/2-inch strips
8 large cloves garlic, chopped
2 tbs. lemon juice
salt and freshly ground pepper to taste
chopped fresh flat-leaf parsley for garnish
grated pecorino cheese, optional

Bring pasta water to boil in a large pot. Add salt and cook pasta according to package directions.

In a small skillet, heat 1 tbs. of the olive oil. Add fresh breadcrumbs and sauté over medium heat, stirring frequently, until golden brown. Season with salt and pepper. Remove from heat and set aside.

Heat a large skillet over medium heat. Sauté pancetta pieces, stirring frequently, until crisp. Remove from skillet. Add 2 tbs. of the olive oil, increase heat to high and add cabbage and garlic. Sauté over high heat until cabbage is lightly browned, about 5 minutes.

Add cooked, drained pasta to skillet with lemon juice. Season with salt and pepper. Toss pasta with cabbage mixture. Distribute remaining 1 tbs. olive oil over finished pasta. Serve immediately on warm plates. Garnish with parsley and toasted breadcrumbs. Pass cheese, if desired.

PASTA WITH SUN-DRIED TOMATOES, MUSHROOMS AND PEAS

Preparation time: 20 minutes
Servings: 3–4

Sun-dried tomatoes provide a terrific taste accent to fresh basil, mushrooms and peas. Add a cup of diced baked ham or turkey ham for a heartier dish.

8 oz. dried small pasta shapes (radiatore, fusilli or orecchiette)
2 tbs. extra virgin olive oil
1 small onion, chopped
8 oz. mushrooms, thinly sliced
5 oz. frozen peas
1/2 cup chicken broth
1/4 cup drained, slivered, oil-packed sun-dried tomatoes
1 tsp. cornstarch dissolved in 1 tbs. dry sherry
salt and freshly ground pepper to taste
1 dash red pepper flakes
1/2 cup grated Parmesan cheese
1/2 cup thinly sliced fresh basil leaves

Cook pasta while making sauce. Heat oil in a large nonstick skillet. Sauté onion for 3 to 4 minutes, until softened. Add mushrooms and turn up heat. Sauté for 3 to 4 minutes. Rinse peas with cold water to defrost. Add chicken stock, peas and sun-dried tomatoes to mushroom mixture. Simmer for 3 to 4 minutes. Stir in cornstarch mixture, salt, pepper and hot pepper flakes. Cook until sauce thickens.

Pour hot, well-drained pasta into skillet. Toss to combine pasta and sauce. Add Parmesan cheese and fresh basil leaves. Serve immediately on warm plates.

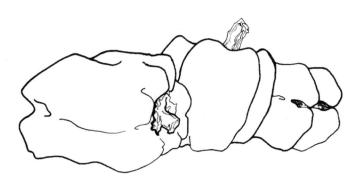

PASTA WITH LENTILS AND PANCETTA

Preparation time: 60 minutes
Servings: 3–4

This is a wonderful, satisfying dish for a rainy evening or when the weather turns crisp and cold. It is also delicious the second day when the flavors have had a chance to develop. Just before serving, top with fresh peeled, seeded, chopped tomato for color and texture contrast.

1/4 cup extra virgin olive oil
1 small onion, diced
1 clove garlic, minced
1 cup dried lentils, picked over and rinsed
1 pkg. (10 oz.) frozen spinach, defrosted and squeezed dry
1 can (14 1/2 oz.) chicken broth
2 cups water
2 tbs. tomato paste

generous amounts freshly ground black pepper
salt to taste
juice of 1/2 lemon
8 oz. dried small pasta shapes (orecchiette or shells)
1 large or 2 small fresh tomatoes, peeled, seeded and chopped
freshly grated Parmesan or Asiago cheese for garnish

Add olive oil to a large saucepan and heat over medium heat. When oil begins to shimmer, add onion and garlic. Reduce heat and cook until onion is translucent, but do not brown garlic. Add lentils and stir to coat with oil. Add squeezed spinach, chicken broth, water and tomato paste and bring to a boil. Reduce heat and simmer for about 25 to 30 minutes, until lentils are almost done and sauce starts to thicken.

When lentils have almost cooked through (about 25 minutes), cook pasta according to package instructions. Add hot, well-drained pasta to simmering sauce; season with salt, pepper and lemon juice. Pour into a warmed bowl, top with chopped tomato and serve immediately. Pass grated cheese.

NEW WORLD VEGETABLE CURRY WITH COUSCOUS

Preparation time: 40 minutes
Servings: 3–4

This colorful dish combines squash, eggplant, yams and corn to make a thick, flavorful topping for couscous or other pasta of your choice. Make this ahead and reheat in the microwave for a quick weekday dinner.

2 tbs. extra virgin olive oil
1 cup chopped onion
2 cloves garlic, minced
1 small hot pepper, minced
1 tbs. curry powder
1½ cups peeled, diced Japanese eggplant, in ½-inch dice
1½ cups peeled, diced yam or sweet potato, in ½-inch dice
2 cups chicken stock
2 small zucchini, cut into ¼-inch slices
2 small yellow squash, cut into ¼-inch slices
kernels from 1 small ear fresh corn
salt and freshly ground pepper to taste

COUSCOUS

1 ½ cups water
2 tbs. vegetable oil
1 cup couscous
salt

Heat olive oil in a large saucepan. Sauté onion, garlic and hot pepper for 3 to 4 minutes, until onion softens. Add curry powder; cook for 1 to 2 minutes. Add egg-plant and cook for 2 minutes. Add yam pieces and chicken stock. Bring to a boil and simmer uncovered for about 10 minutes. Stir in squashes and cook for 10 minutes. Add corn, salt and pepper. Cook for 5 minutes.

Cook couscous: Bring water and oil to boil in a large nonstick skillet. Add couscous and salt, cover, remove from heat and let stand for 5 minutes. Uncover and fluff grains with a fork.

Serve in heated shallow bowls. Place a large scoop of couscous in bowl and top with about 1 cup curry sauce per serving.

PASTA WITH CHINESE CABBAGE AND BLACK MUSHROOMS

Preparation time: 30 minutes
Servings: 3–4

This full-flavored pasta dish features all the wonderful flavors of Chinese food. Dried black mushrooms are softened, slivered, and sautéed with fresh mushrooms, crisp Napa cabbage and onions.

8 small dried Asian black mushrooms
6–7 cups thinly sliced Napa cabbage, in 1/4-inch slivers
8 oz. dried pasta (fusilli or gemellini)
3 tbs. vegetable oil
2 tsp. minced fresh ginger
1 medium onion, thinly sliced
8 oz. fresh mushrooms, thinly sliced
1 pinch red pepper flakes
2 tbs. soy sauce
1 can (14 1/2 oz.) beef broth
2 tbs. sesame oil
2 tbs. cornstarch dissolved in 3 tbs. water

Cover dried mushrooms with warm water and let stand for about 20 minutes. Squeeze dry and cut out tough center stem. Cut into thin slivers. Bring pasta water to a boil.

Heat vegetable oil in a large sauté pan. Sauté minced ginger for 1 minute. Add onion and fresh mushrooms. Sauté for 3 to 4 minutes over high heat. Add drained slivered black mushrooms, red pepper flakes, soy sauce and beef broth and bring to a boil. Simmer for about 5 minutes. Add cabbage and cook for 1 to 2 minutes, until cabbage softens. Stir in a little dissolved cornstarch to thicken sauce, using just enough to make a glaze but not thick sauce. Add hot, well-drained pasta to skillet and toss. Pour into a warm serving bowl. Serve immediately.

PASTA TUBES WITH EGGPLANT AND GARLIC

Preparation time: 40 minutes
Servings: 3–4

Use long, purple Asian eggplants for this classic pasta dish. Broiling the eggplant first reduces the amount of oil it absorbs and makes a lighter dish.

10 oz. gemellini or other dried hollow pasta tubes
4–5 Asian eggplants, about 1 lb.
1/4 cup extra virgin olive oil, divided
1 small onion, chopped
4 cloves garlic, minced
1/4 tsp. red pepper flakes
1 can (14 1/2 oz.) ready-cut tomatoes with juice
2 tsp. anchovy paste
1/4 cup finely chopped fresh basil, or 2 tsp. dried
salt and freshly ground black pepper to taste
chopped fresh basil or flat-leaf parsley for garnish
freshly grated pecorino or Parmesan cheese for garnish

Heat broiler. Trim eggplants and cut into ½-inch slices lengthwise. Brush both sides of slices with about 2 tbs. of the oil and place on a cookie sheet. Broil for 3 to 4 minutes per side, or until eggplant slices are lightly browned and tender. Remove from broiler, let stand until cool enough to handle and cut crosswise into 1-inch pieces. Heat remaining oil in a large skillet and sauté onion for 5 to 6 minutes to soften. Add garlic and red pepper flakes and cook for another minute. Add tomatoes with juice, anchovy paste, basil and eggplant pieces. Simmer over medium heat for 10 minutes. Season with salt and pepper.

While making sauce, bring pasta water to boil in a large pot. Add salt and cook pasta according to package directions. Pour hot, drained pasta into skillet, toss to combine, cook for another minute and serve immediately on warm plates. If pasta sauce seems too thick, add 2 to 3 tbs. pasta cooking water to thin. Garnish with basil and pass cheese.

Wine suggestion: a fruity Zinfandel or Barbera

PENNE WITH FENNEL
AND ROASTED RED PEPPERS

Preparation time: 30 minutes
Servings: 3–4

Anise-flavored fennel strips cook with the pasta and are tossed with roasted red pepper pieces and grated Gruyère cheese. Garnish pasta servings with some of the fine fennel fronds.

8 oz. dried penne noodles
2 medium bulbs fennel
2 tbs. butter
1/2 cup chopped onion
2 cloves garlic, minced
1/4 tsp. hot pepper flakes
3 tbs. heavy cream
1/2 cup roasted red pepper or pimiento strips
3/4 cup coarsely grated Gruyère cheese
salt and freshly ground pepper to taste
fennel fronds and grated Parmesan cheese for garnish

Heat pasta water. Cut tops from fennel bulbs and reserve. Trim root ends. Discard any tough or damaged outer fennel pieces. Cut bulb in half from top to root end. Place cut-side down and, starting at the root end, cut into $3/8$-inch slices. Add fennel strips to boiling pasta after pasta has cooked for 2 minutes.

Heat butter in a large nonstick skillet. Sauté onions and garlic over medium heat for 3 to 4 minutes, until onions have softened. Add hot pepper flakes, cream and roasted peppers. Cook over low heat for 2 to 3 minutes to blend flavors. Pour hot, well-drained pasta and fennel into skillet. Add Gruyère, salt and pepper. Toss to combine. Serve immediately on warm plates. Garnish with finely chopped fennel fronds and pass Parmesan cheese.

PASTA WITH SNOW PEAS AND MUSHROOMS

Preparation time: 30 minutes
Servings: 3–4

Crisp green snow peas are paired with dried black mushrooms for a tasty pasta dish. The snow peas will cook with the pasta for a minute before pasta is done. If you wish, sugar snap peas can be substituted for snow peas.

4–5 dried Asian black mushrooms, softened in warm water for 20 minutes
8 oz. dried pasta (fusilli, gemellini or penne)
8 oz. snow peas, stemmed and cut into ½-inch strips
2 tbs. vegetable oil
4–6 green onions, including 1 inch green part, thinly sliced
1 cup chicken broth
¼ cup dry sherry
1 tsp. cornstarch dissolved in 2 tbs. water
1 tsp. toasted sesame oil
salt and freshly ground pepper to taste
1 medium tomato, peeled, seeded and chopped
grated Parmesan cheese, optional

Cover dried mushrooms with warm water to soften while preparing remaining ingredients. Drain softened mushrooms and squeeze until very dry. Remove tough center stem and cut into very thin strips. Bring pasta water to a boil and add pasta. One minute before pasta has finished cooking, add snow peas to water.

In a large nonstick skillet, sauté onions in oil for 3 to 4 minutes to soften. Add mushroom strips, chicken broth and sherry; bring to a boil and cook for 2 to 3 minutes. Add sesame oil, salt and pepper.

Pour hot, well-drained pasta and peas into skillet and toss to combine. Bring to a boil. If sauce is very thin, thicken with some of the dissolved cornstarch. Pour into a warm serving bowl, top with chopped tomato and serve immediately on warm plates. Pass Parmesan cheese, if desired.

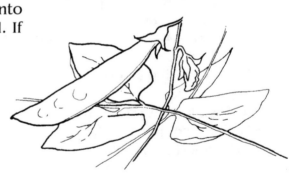

LINGUINE WITH BLACK BEANS AND CARAMELIZED ONIONS

Preparation time: 30 minutes
Servings: 3–4

Black beans and sweet cooked onions are paired with pasta for a hearty main dish.

2 tbs. extra virgin olive oil
2 large onions, cut into 1/2-inch slices (about 1 lb.)
1 clove garlic
1 large jalapeño chile pepper, stemmed, seeded, chopped
1 can (15 oz.) tomato sauce
1 can (15 1/2 oz.) black beans, rinsed and drained
1 tsp. dried oregano
1/3 cup slivered oil-packed sun-dried tomatoes
1 tbs. lemon juice
salt and freshly ground pepper to taste
12 oz. dried linguine
1/4 cup chopped fresh cilantro for garnish
freshly grated pecorino or Parmesan cheese

Heat oil in a large skillet, add onions and sauté over medium heat for 2 to 3 minutes. Add 2 tbs. water to skillet and lower heat. Cover and cook for 15 minutes, stirring occasionally. Remove lid, increase heat and continue to cook for another 5 minutes, or until onions are lightly browned. Add garlic and jalapeño and cook for 1 minute. Add tomato sauce, bring to a boil and simmer for 2 to 3 minutes. Add black beans, oregano, tomatoes and lemon juice and heat through. Season to taste with salt and pepper.

While making sauce, bring pasta cooking water to boil in a large pot and cook pasta. Add hot, well-drained pasta to sauce in skillet. Toss to combine. Add 2 to 3 tbs. cheese. Serve immediately on warm plates, garnish with cilantro and pass extra cheese.

ORZO WITH CURRIED CAULIFLOWER SAUCE

Preparation time: 30 minutes
Servings: 3–4

The small orzo pasta is in the shape of large grains of rice and makes a fine base for this curry sauce. Serve a mango chutney or your favorite fruit salsa with the curry. Cook cauliflower in the boiling pasta water before adding the pasta.

4 cups cauliflower florets, about 12 oz.
10 oz. dried orzo or small pasta shells
3 tbs. butter
1 cup chopped onion
1 tbs. Madras curry powder
1 tbs. flour
1 can (14½ oz.) chicken broth
2 tbs. tomato paste
1 large tomato, peeled, seeded and coarsely
    chopped
1 tbs. lemon juice
salt and freshly ground pepper
⅓ cup coarsely chopped dry-roasted peanuts
mango chutney to taste

Heat pasta water in a large pot. When boiling, add salt and cauliflower florets and cook for 5 to 6 minutes, until tender. Remove cauliflower from pot with a strainer, drain and set aside on a plate or pie tin. Add orzo to pot and cook for about 9 minutes or according to package directions.

While pasta water is heating, melt butter in a large nonstick skillet. Sauté onion over medium heat for 5 to 8 minutes, until soft and translucent. Add curry powder and flour and cook for 2 minutes. Gradually stir in chicken broth and tomato paste. Bring to a boil and cook for 2 to 3 minutes. Reserve a few cooked cauliflower florets and coarsely mash remaining cauliflower with a fork. Add both whole and mashed cauliflower pieces, tomato and lemon juice to saucepan. Season to taste with salt and pepper and continue to cook sauce over low heat until pasta is done.

Drain orzo and add to skillet with sauce. Stir to combine. Serve immediately on warm plates and sprinkle with chopped peanuts. Pass mango chutney.

CONFETTI PASTA

Preparation time: 30 minutes
Servings: 3–4

Fresh red and yellow peppers make this a colorful pasta dish. Peeling the fresh peppers with a vegetable peeler results in a crisp, crunchy texture very different from roasted peppers, and is worth the effort.

12 oz. fresh pasta, or 8 oz. dried
1 red bell pepper
1 yellow bell pepper
2 tbs. extra virgin olive oil
1 small onion, chopped
2 cloves garlic, minced
1/2 cup green peas, fresh or defrosted
1/4 cup chopped black olives
1/2 tsp. dried oregano

1/2 tsp. dried basil, or 3 tbs. chopped fresh
3 tbs. chopped fresh flat-leaf parsley
1 cup cubed fontina or other mild cheese, in 1/4-inch cubes
freshly ground black pepper
salt to taste
freshly grated pecorino cheese

Heat pasta water. Cut peppers into vertical sections following the natural ridges. Remove seeds and membranes. Using a vegetable peeler, remove thin outer skin. Cut into ¼-inch strips.

Begin cooking pasta. Heat olive oil in a medium skillet. Sauté onion and garlic for 3 to 4 minutes, until soft but not brown. Add peppers and cook for 1 minute. Stir in peas, olives, oregano, basil, parsley, cheese, salt and pepper. Pour hot, well-drained pasta into skillet and toss to combine. Serve immediately on warm plates. Pass cheese.

Variation: Add 1 cup diced ham, prosciutto or smoked turkey breast.

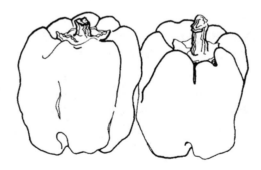

PASTA WITH FRESH ZUCCHINI

Preparation time: 30 minutes
Servings: 3–4

Here is a flavorful zucchini and tomato topping for pasta that will appeal even to people who don't like zucchini.

12 oz. fresh pasta, or 8 oz. dried
2 tbs. extra virgin olive oil
1 medium onion, chopped
1 clove garlic, minced
3 medium zucchini, about 1 lb.
1 can (15 oz.) tomato sauce
1 tsp. dried marjoram

$1/2$ tsp. dried basil
$1/2$ tsp. salt
$1/4$ tsp. white pepper
2–3 drops Tabasco Sauce
freshly grated Parmesan cheese for
  topping

Begin heating pasta cooking water. Heat oil in a large skillet. Sauté onion until soft but not brown. Add garlic. Slice zucchini in half lengthwise and then slice across into $1/2$-inch slices. Add to onion and garlic. Stir in tomato sauce with marjoram and basil. Cover and simmer for 10 minutes, stirring occasionally. Cook pasta. Pour hot, well-drained pasta into skillet and toss to combine. Serve immediately on heated plates. Pass freshly grated Parmesan cheese.

PASTA PROVENÇAL

Preparation time: 15 minutes
Servings: 3–4

Crisp eggplant and red pepper slivers make a quick, savory first course or luncheon dish.

12 oz. fresh pasta, or 8 oz. dried
2 Japanese eggplants, unpeeled
flour for dusting
$\frac{1}{4}$ cup extra virgin olive oil
1 red pepper, peeled and cut into thin
  strips

3 cloves garlic, minced
salt and freshly ground pepper
2 tbs. chopped fresh flat-leaf parsley
grated Parmesan cheese for topping

Heat pasta water. Time pasta so it is cooked when sauce is ready. Trim eggplants and cut in quarters lengthwise and then cut quarters into $\frac{1}{4}$-inch slices crosswise. Lightly dust eggplant pieces with flour. Heat oil in a large skillet. When oil shimmers, add eggplant and sauté over medium heat for about 3 minutes, until lightly browned. Add eggplant, red pepper, garlic, salt and pepper. Sauté for another 2 to 3 minutes, until eggplant is crisp and lightly browned. Pour hot, well-drained pasta into skillet and toss to combine. If pasta seems a little dry, add 1 or 2 tbs. pasta cooking water. Pass cheese.

PASTA PRIMAVERA

Preparation time: 30 minutes
Servings: 3–4

With lots of fresh vegetables, this Italian classic is as healthful as it is delicious.

8 oz. dried spaghetti, tagliarini or fettuccine, or 12 oz. fresh
$1/4$ cup extra virgin olive oil
1 small onion, finely chopped
2 small tomatoes, peeled, seeded, and coarsely chopped
$1/4$ tsp. red pepper flakes
$1/2$ lb. mushrooms, thinly sliced
1 clove garlic, minced
1 cup diagonally sliced asparagus or green beans, in $1/2$-inch slices
1 cup cauliflower florets
1 medium yellow squash, thinly sliced
1 red or yellow bell pepper, peeled and cut into thin strips
1 cup coarsely grated carrots
$1/2$ cup fresh blanched or frozen green peas
salt and freshly ground black pepper
3 tbs. finely chopped fresh flat-leaf parsley or finely sliced fresh basil
freshly grated Parmesan cheese

Heat pasta water. Time pasta so it is cooked when the sauce is finished. Heat olive oil in a large skillet. Over medium heat, sauté onion and tomatoes for 3 to 4 minutes. Add red pepper flakes, mushrooms and garlic, and cook for 2 minutes. Add asparagus, cauliflower, squash and peppers, cover and cook for 2 minutes. Add carrots, tomato pieces, peas, salt and pepper, and continue to cook for 2 to 3 minutes. Add hot, well-drained pasta to skillet and toss to combine. Top with parsley and serve immediately on warm plates. Pass Parmesan cheese.

BROCCOLI AND BOWTIE PASTA

Preparation time: 30 minutes
Servings: 3–4

Broccoli florets team up with whimsical bowtie-shaped pasta (farfalle) to make an attractive, nutritious luncheon or supper dish. Use broccoli stems for soup or a stir-fry. Add broccoli to cooking pasta for last 5 minutes of pasta cooking time.

1 bunch broccoli, florets only
8 oz. dried bowtie pasta (farfalle)
1 tbs. extra virgin olive oil
2 large cloves garlic, minced
1/4 tsp. red pepper flakes
salt and freshly ground pepper

3 tbs. oil-packed sun-dried tomato pieces,
    or 2 tbs. sun-dried tomato paste
1/2 cup heavy cream
1/4 cup grated Parmesan cheese
1/4 cup pine nuts, toasted
grated Parmesan cheese for garnish

Prepare broccoli, cutting thicker florets in half. Pieces should be about thumb size. Cook pasta according to package directions. Five minutes before pasta is done, add broccoli to cooking water. Heat olive oil in a large skillet. Sauté garlic and red pepper flakes for 1 to 2 minutes. Add cream, bring to boil and cook for 2 to 3 minutes, until sauce starts to thicken. Pour hot, well-drained pasta and broccoli into skillet. Add salt, pepper, tomato pieces and Parmesan cheese. Toss well. Top with toasted pine nuts. Serve immediately on warm plates. Pass additional grated cheese.

Variation: Add 1 cup smoked turkey strips to hot pasta.

PASTA WITH SEAFOOD

Seafood and pasta are another natural alliance. There are probably as many different varieties of seafood available as there are pasta shapes.

Always choose the freshest seafood available because anything less will detract from the dish. It is important not to cook fish or shellfish too long. Seafood needs cooking only to firm its flesh. To avoid overcooking, most of the following recipes call for adding the fish or shellfish when the sauce is almost done, or sautéing it separately and then combining with the pasta just before serving.

PENNE WITH ASPARAGUS AND SHRIMP

Preparation time: 30 minutes
Servings: 3–4

Use penne (quill-shaped pasta) and cut the asparagus on the diagonal to match the penne in shape. A quick way to blanch the asparagus is to add it to the pasta pot for the last 2 minutes before the pasta is done and then drain the pasta and asparagus at the same time.

8 oz. dried penne
2 cups asparagus (about 8 oz. trimmed)
1 tbs. olive oil
6 green onions, including 1 inch green part, thinly sliced
$3/4$ lb. uncooked small shrimp, peeled and deveined
$1/4$ cup plain yogurt
$1/4$ cup heavy cream
salt and freshly ground pepper to taste
$1/4$ tsp. dried tarragon
1 tbs. lemon juice
2 tbs. finely chopped fresh flat-leaf parsley

Begin heating pasta water in a large pot. Cut trimmed asparagus into thin diagonal slices about the same size as penne and set aside. Heat olive oil in a large non-stick skillet. Sauté onions over low heat for 2 to 3 minutes, until translucent. Add shrimp and cook over medium heat until they start to turn pink. Add yogurt, cream, salt, pepper, tarragon and lemon juice. Cook for 1 to 2 minutes, until mixture is hot, but not boiling. Cook pasta according to package directions. Two minutes before pasta is done, add asparagus pieces to cooking water. Pour hot, well-drained pasta and asparagus into skillet with sauce. Toss to mix well. Garnish with parsley. Serve immediately on warm plates.

LARGE SHELLS STUFFED WITH SHRIMP

Preparation time: 20 minutes
Makes: 12 shells

These light appetizers go beautifully with a crisp Orvieto wine, or a dry riesling. Serve them as part of a luncheon or picnic plate with ripe red tomatoes and a vegetable salad. Cook a couple of extra shells in case one or two split during cooking.

12–15 dried jumbo pasta shells
1 lb. small cooked salad shrimp
4 green onions, thinly sliced
1/4 cup finely diced celery
1/4 cup finely minced fresh flat-leaf
  parsley

2 tsp. lemon juice
2 tbs. finely chopped oil-packed
  sun-dried tomato pieces
1 tbs. cream cheese
1 tbs. mayonnaise
salt and finely ground white pepper

Cook pasta shells according to package directions. Drain and rinse with cold water to prevent sticking and to cool before stuffing. Reserve 12 small whole shrimp for garnish. If shrimp are 1 to 1 1/2 inches in size, cut each in half. Combine remaining ingredients and mix lightly with a fork. Fill pasta shells with a small spoon and refrigerate until ready to serve. Remove from refrigerator 20 minutes before serving. Garnish each shell with a reserved whole shrimp. These are best when used the same day you make them.

ANGEL HAIR PASTA WITH BAY SCALLOPS

Preparation time: 20 minutes
Servings: 2 dinner or 4 appetizer

Tender strands of pasta accented with lemon, delicate bay scallops, and fresh basil make an elegant first course or dinner for two.

1/2 lb. bay scallops
4 oz. dried angel hair or capellini pasta
1 tbs. butter
3–4 green onions, including 1 inch green part, thinly sliced
grated zest of 1 lemon

2 tbs. lemon juice
3 tbs. heavy cream
salt and white pepper to taste
2 tbs. thinly sliced fresh basil or chopped fresh flat-leaf parsley

Wash scallops and remove tiny, tough muscle on each side of scallop. Bring pasta water to a boil. Melt butter in a large nonstick skillet over medium heat. Sauté onions for 2 to 3 minutes, until translucent. Add scallops and cook for 1 to 2 minutes, until they turn opaque. Stir in lemon zest and juice. Let stand until pasta is cooked. Just before pasta is done, add cream, salt and pepper to skillet and bring to a boil. Add hot, well-drained pasta to skillet and toss to combine. Serve immediately on warm plates. Garnish with fresh basil or parsley.

RIGATONI WITH ZESTY TUNA SAUCE

Preparation time: 30 minutes
Servings: 3–4

Fresh tuna pieces simmered in a hearty tomato sauce make a satisfying dinner. Serve with a fresh green salad and some crisp garlic bread.

3 tbs. extra virgin olive oil
1/2 cup chopped onion
2 cloves garlic, minced
1 dash red pepper flakes
1 can (14 1/2 oz.) ready-cut tomatoes
   with juice
2 tbs. tomato paste
1/4 cup dry white wine
2 anchovy fillets, rinsed and chopped

1/2 cup pitted, coarsely chopped
   kalamata olives
1 tbs. balsamic or red wine vinegar
1 lb. fresh tuna, cut into 3/4-inch pieces
salt and freshly ground pepper to taste
8 oz. dried rigatoni noodles
chopped fresh flat-leaf parsley for
   garnish
grated Parmesan cheese, optional

Heat oil in a large skillet. Sauté onion for 3 to 4 minutes, until softened. Add garlic, red pepper flakes, tomatoes, tomato paste and wine. Cook for 5 to 7 minutes, until juices thicken slightly. Add anchovies, olives, vinegar, tuna pieces, salt and pepper. Simmer for 3 to 4 minutes, until tuna pieces are cooked through. Cook pasta. Add hot, well-drained pasta to skillet. Toss and serve immediately on warm plates. Garnish with parsley. Pass cheese if desired.

PASTA WITH SCALLOPS AND RED PEPPERS

Preparation time: 30 minutes
Servings: 3–4

Vibrant red bell peppers provide a pleasant contrast to pasta and scallops in both flavor and appearance. Use a vegetable peeler to peel the peppers.

1 lb. scallops, cut in half if large
12 oz. fresh pasta (fettuccine or
  rigatoni), or 8 oz. dried
2 medium red bell peppers, peeled
2 tbs. butter

3 tbs. minced shallots
1 cup heavy cream
$1/4$ tsp. white pepper
salt to taste
2 tbs. minced fresh flat-leaf parsley

This sauce can be made quickly, so time pasta to be done about 6 minutes after you begin cooking the sauce. Wash scallops, remove tough muscle on sides and pat dry. Cut peppers into thin slivers.

Melt butter in a large skillet. Sauté shallots for 1 minute and add cream and white pepper. Turn heat to high and reduce cream for 2 to 3 minutes, until it starts to thicken. Reduce heat to medium and add scallops and salt. Cook for 1 minute. Add red peppers and cook for 1 minute. Add hot, well-drained pasta to skillet, toss and stir to combine. Serve immediately on warm plates. Garnish with parsley.

PASTA WITH SHRIMP AND DILL SAUCE

Preparation time: 30 minutes
Servings: 3–4

This delicate sauce is lightly flavored with dill. Use fettuccine or wider egg noodles.

12 oz. fresh pasta, or 8 oz. dried
3/4 cup plain yogurt
1/4 cup heavy cream
1 tbs. soy sauce
1 tsp. Worcestershire sauce
1/2 tsp. dry mustard
1/2 tsp. dried dill weed, or 1 tbs. finely chopped fresh dill
1/4 tsp. white pepper
1/2 lb. small cooked salad shrimp

Cook pasta while making sauce. Gently heat yogurt, cream, soy sauce, Worcestershire, mustard, dill and pepper. Do not allow to boil. Add shrimp and heat through. Add hot, well-drained pasta to skillet and toss to combine. Serve immediately on warm plates.

Wine suggestion: Chardonnay or Sauvignon blanc

PASTA WITH CRAB

Preparation time: 30 minutes
Servings: 3–4

Use green fettuccine for this quick and pretty seafood pasta.

12 oz. fresh pasta, or 8 oz. dried
3 tbs. butter
2 tbs. minced shallots
6–8 mushrooms, sliced
1/2 tsp. grated fresh ginger
3 oz. cream cheese, cut into small cubes

1/2 cup half-and-half
1 1/2 cups cooked flaked crabmeat
dash cayenne pepper
salt and freshly ground pepper to taste
2 tbs. minced fresh flat-leaf parsley for garnish

Have pasta cooking water at a boil and time pasta to be done when sauce is ready. Melt butter in a large skillet. When foaming, add shallots, mushrooms and fresh ginger. Sauté for 3 to 4 minutes, until mushroom liquid is released. Add cream cheese and half-and-half. Increase heat and cook for 2 to 3 minutes, until sauce starts to thicken. Add crabmeat, cayenne pepper, salt and pepper. Cook only until crab is warmed through, breaking up pieces as little as possible. Add hot, well-drained pasta to skillet and toss to combine. Serve immediately on warm plates. Garnish with parsley.

Wine suggestion: Pinot blanc or dry Semillon

PASTA WITH SALMON AND SPRING VEGETABLES

Preparation time: 30 minutes
Servings: 3–4

Colorful vegetables and chunks of fresh pink salmon make a delicious main course. Time the pasta so you have about 4 minutes to cook the vegetables and salmon pieces before the pasta is done.

8 oz. dried corkscrew or radiatore pasta
2 tbs. butter
3 tbs. finely chopped shallots
1 cup clam juice
1 tbs. lemon juice
1/2 cup heavy cream
2 small carrots, thinly sliced in rounds
1 small zucchini, thinly sliced in rounds
2 tbs. fresh dill, or 1 tbs. fresh thyme leaves, or 1/2 tsp. dried herbs
salt and freshly ground pepper to taste
1 lb. salmon, cut into 3/4-inch pieces
1/2 cup frozen peas, rinsed with cold water to defrost
1 1/2 cups cherry tomatoes, cut into halves or quarters

Bring pasta water to a boil. Cook pasta according to package directions. Melt butter in a large skillet and sauté shallots 1 to 2 minutes. Add clam juice and lemon juice. Turn heat to high and reduce volume by about half. Lower heat, add cream and simmer for 2 to 3 minutes. About 4 minutes before pasta is done, add carrots, zucchini, dill, salt and pepper to cream mixture. Cook over medium heat for about 2 minutes. Add salmon pieces and peas. Cook for 1 to 2 minutes, turning salmon pieces so they cook evenly. Add tomatoes. Pour hot, well-drained pasta into skillet and toss gently with sauce. Serve immediately on heated plates.

Wine suggestion: dry Riesling or Sauvignon blanc

LINGUINE WITH CURRIED MUSSELS

Preparation time: 40 minutes
Servings: 3–4

The delicate curry flavor is delightful with both pasta and mussels. Clams are also delicious in this dish.

8 oz. dried linguine noodles, or 12 oz. fresh
3–4 dozen mussels
5 tbs. extra virgin olive oil, divided
1/4 tsp. dried red pepper flakes
1/2 cup dry white wine or vermouth
1/4 cup heavy cream
1 large onion, thinly sliced
1 large clove garlic, minced
1 1/2 tsp. curry powder
1 cup fresh tomato pieces
salt and freshly ground pepper to taste

Have pasta cooking water boiling and time pasta to be done when the sauce is ready. Scrub mussels with a stiff brush and remove any beards. Heat 2 tbs. of the olive oil in a large skillet or heavy pot. Add pepper flakes and sauté for 1 minute. Add mussels and wine. Cover pot and cook over high heat for 3 to 4 minutes, or until shells have opened. Shake pan occasionally while mussels are steaming. Remove from heat and let cool. When cool enough to handle, remove mussels from opened shells. Discard any shells that have not opened. Reserve several shells for garnishing plates or serving bowl. Strain 3/4 cup mussel liquid through cheesecloth or a paper coffee filter into a measuring cup. Add heavy cream.

Heat remaining 3 tbs. olive oil in a large skillet. Add onion slices and cook until onion is soft and translucent but not browned. Add garlic and curry powder to onion and cook for 2 minutes. Add tomato pieces, mussel juice and cream mixture, salt and pepper. Cook over high heat for 3 to 4 minutes, until sauce starts to thicken. Add mussels and just heat through.

Pour hot, well-drained pasta into skillet and toss to combine with sauce. Serve immediately on heated plates. Garnish with reserved mussel shells.

Wine suggestion: Chenin blanc or Gewürztraminer

BOWTIE PASTA WITH FISH, VERACRUZ-STYLE

Preparation time: 30 minutes
Servings: 4–5

The hearty flavors of tomato and red pepper complement sea bass, rock cod or other firm-fleshed fish. Serve in shallow soup plates with crusty French bread to finish off the sauce.

8 oz. dried bowtie pasta (farfalle) or sea shells (conchiglie), or 12 oz. fresh
2 tbs. extra virgin olive oil
1 small onion, finely chopped
1 large red bell pepper, peeled, seeded and chopped
1 large clove garlic, minced
1 tbs. anchovy paste
$1/2$ tsp. red pepper flakes, or 1 small fresh hot pepper, diced
1 large can (28 oz.) ready-cut tomatoes
1 lb. sea bass or rock cod, cut into 1-inch pieces
grated zest and juice of 1 orange
1 tbs. lemon juice
salt and freshly ground pepper to taste

Heat pasta water and time pasta to be done when sauce is ready. Heat oil in a large skillet. Add onion and cook for 4 to 5 minutes, until soft but not brown. Add red pepper, garlic, anchovy paste and red pepper flakes. Cook over low heat for 2 minutes. Add tomatoes and cook over high heat for 3 to 4 minutes, breaking up large pieces of tomato. Add fish, orange zest, orange and lemon juices to pan. Simmer gently for 2 to 3 minutes, until fish is just done. Do not overcook. Add hot, well-drained pasta to skillet and toss to combine. Serve immediately in heated shallow soup bowls.

Wine suggestion: rosé or Sauvignon Blanc

SHRIMP CHOW MEIN

This classic Chinese dish goes together very quickly after the shrimp are prepared and the vegetables sliced. Thinly sliced cabbage can be substituted for the bean sprouts.

6 oz. fresh Chinese noodles, or 4 oz. dried spaghettini
2 tbs. cornstarch
1 tbs. plus 1 tsp. soy sauce
1 egg white
1/4 tsp. white pepper
6 oz. small uncooked shrimp, peeled, deveined and cut in half lengthwise
6 tbs. vegetable oil
1 large clove garlic, peeled and flattened
1/4-inch slice fresh ginger
3 green onions, including 1 inch green part, thinly sliced
6 oz. small mushrooms, thinly sliced
6 oz. fresh bean sprouts
1 tsp. toasted sesame oil

Cook noodles and drain. Cover with cool water to keep from sticking together. Combine cornstarch, 1 tsp. of the soy sauce, egg white and white pepper. Pour over shrimp, mix well and set aside.

Heat 2 tbs. of the oil in a wok or large nonstick skillet over high heat. Add garlic and ginger. Cook for 1 minute, until slightly brown, then remove and discard. Add drained, cooked noodles to skillet. Stir to coat with oil and lightly brown on all sides. Turn out onto a plate. Add 2 tbs. more oil to skillet. When hot, add shrimp mixture. Stir quickly for 1 to 2 minutes, until shrimp are opaque and firm. Turn shrimp out onto another plate.

Add remaining 2 tbs. vegetable oil to skillet. When hot, add onion and mushrooms and stir-fry for 1 to 2 minutes. Add bean sprouts and toss quickly. Return shrimp and cooked noodles to skillet and toss. Remove from heat and sprinkle with remaining 1 tbs. soy sauce and sesame oil. Stir quickly and serve immediately on warm plates.

Wine suggestion: Chenin blanc or dry Riesling

Variation: Uncooked chicken cut into ½-inch cubes can be substituted for the shrimp.

LINGUINE WITH
WHITE CLAM SAUCE

Preparation time: 30 minutes
Servings: 4–5

Clams cooked with white wine and garlic make a delicious classic pasta sauce. Strain clam juice through a coffee filter to get rid of any sand.

1 lb. fresh linguine noodles, or
  12 oz. dried
1/4 cup butter
2 cloves garlic, minced
2 tbs. flour
2 cans (6 1/2 oz. each) chopped clams

1/4 cup dry white wine or dry vermouth
half-and-half
1/4 cup finely chopped fresh flat-leaf
  parsley
1/2 tsp. dried thyme
salt and freshly ground pepper to taste

Heat pasta water. Melt butter in a small saucepan. Add garlic to butter and cook for 1 minute. Stir in flour and cook for 2 minutes. Drain clam juice into a paper coffee filter set in a 2-cup measure to catch any sand or shell. Discard filter and add white wine and enough half-and-half to make 2 cups liquid. Gradually stir liquid into flour mixture and cook until sauce thickens slightly. Add parsley, thyme, salt and pepper. Simmer for about 10 minutes. Add clams to sauce and heat to serving temperature. Pour into a heated bowl and combine with hot, well-drained pasta. Serve immediately on warm plates.

PASTA WITH POULTRY AND MEAT

Pasta pairs well with all kinds of poultry and meats, and there is no limit to the savory combinations you can make. Deli-style turkey hams, smoked turkey sausages and meats provide lower-fat alternatives with a lot of hearty flavor.

PASTA WITH CHICKEN, ORANGE AND TOMATO SAUCE

Preparation time: 30 minutes
Servings: 3–4

A zesty orange and tomato sauce coats mushrooms and tender pieces of chicken to make this easy pasta sauce.

3 tbs. olive oil, divided
4 boneless, skinless chicken thighs, cut into 1-inch chunks, about 10 oz.
flour seasoned with salt, pepper and cayenne pepper to coat chicken pieces
1 cup diced onion
1/2 tsp. red pepper flakes
1/2 lb. medium mushrooms, trimmed and cut into quarters
6–8 pieces sun-dried tomatoes, cut into halves
grated zest of 1 orange
2/3 cup orange juice
8 oz. tomato sauce
2/3 cup dry white wine
1 tsp. dried tarragon
10 oz. dried orecchiette or other small pasta shapes
salt and freshly ground pepper to taste
chopped fresh flat-leaf parsley for garnish

In a large skillet, heat 2 tbs. olive oil over medium-high heat. Dredge chicken pieces in seasoned flour. Sauté chicken in hot olive oil until nicely browned on all sides. Remove from the pan with a slotted spoon and set aside. Add remaining olive oil to skillet and add onions, red pepper flakes and mushrooms. Sauté over medium heat until onions are soft, about 5 to 6 minutes. Return chicken pieces to skillet. Add tomatoes, orange zest, orange juice, tomato sauce, white wine and tarragon. Cook over medium heat for 15 minutes, until chicken is cooked through and sauce is slightly reduced.

While chicken is cooking, bring pasta water to boil in a large pot. Cook pasta according to package directions. Drain pasta and add to skillet with chicken; stir to combine. Season with salt and pepper and garnish with parsley. Serve immediately on warm plates.

PENNE WITH SMOKED CHICKEN AND ARUGULA

Preparation time: 30 minutes
Servings: 3–4

This attractive and flavorful pasta sauce goes together quickly. Substitute smoked turkey breast if you wish.

10 oz. dried penne
1 pinch salt for pasta water
2 tbs. extra virgin olive oil
$1/2$ cup chopped onion
$1/2$ lb. thinly sliced mushrooms
$1/4$ tsp. red pepper flakes
$1/2$ cup chicken broth
2 tbs. heavy cream
$1/3$ cup oil-packed sun-dried tomato pieces, coarsely chopped
6 oz. smoked chicken breast, cut into $1/2$ inch cubes
3 cups coarsely chopped arugula leaves
salt and freshly ground pepper to taste
freshly grated Parmesan cheese

Bring pasta cooking water to boil in a large pot. Add salt and cook pasta according to package directions.

Heat olive oil over medium-high heat in a large nonstick skillet. Sauté onion, mushrooms and red pepper flakes for 6 to 8 minutes, until soft. Add chicken stock and cream and bring to a boil. Add tomato pieces and chicken, lower heat and cook for 2 minutes to heat through. Season to taste.

Drain cooked pasta and add pasta and arugula to skillet. Gently toss pasta with sauce to combine. If pasta seems dry, add 1 to 2 tbs. chicken broth or pasta cooking water. Serve immediately on warm plates. Pass Parmesan cheese.

Wine suggestion: rosé or Merlot

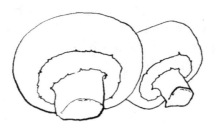

BOWTIE PASTA WITH CHICKEN AND TURKEY SAUSAGE

Preparation time: 30 minutes
Servings: 3–4

Tender nuggets of chicken and mild turkey sausages are paired with bowties to make a delicious hearty pasta main course.

3 turkey or mild Italian pork sausages
1/4 cup dry wine
3 boneless, skinless chicken breast halves
flour, salt and pepper to coat chicken
2 tbs. butter
3 tbs. minced shallots
1 cup chicken broth
1/2 cup peeled, seeded, chopped tomatoes
2–3 tbs. coarsely chopped roasted pepper or pimiento
salt and freshly ground pepper to taste
8 oz. dried bowtie pasta (farfalle) or fettuccine
2 tbs. chopped fresh flat-leaf parsley

Place sausages and white wine in a small saucepan. Cover, bring to a boil and simmer for 5 minutes. Uncover and prick sausages to release fat. Increase heat to evaporate liquid and lightly brown sausages. Remove from pan and, when cool enough to handle, cut into 1/2-inch-thick rounds. Cut chicken breasts into 1-inch pieces. Dust lightly with seasoned flour.

Melt butter in a large skillet over medium heat. When foaming, add chicken and sauté until lightly browned, about 2 minutes on each side. Remove from pan. Reduce heat to low and add shallots. Stir for 1 minute. Add chicken broth and stir to remove browned bits from bottom of pan. Bring to a boil. Add chicken pieces, sausages, tomato, roasted pepper, salt and pepper. Heat through. Cook pasta. Pour hot, well-drained pasta into skillet and toss to combine. Serve immediately on warm plates. Garnish with parsley.

MACARONI AND CHICKEN PUNJAB-STYLE

Preparation time: 30 minutes
Baking time: 20 minutes
Servings: 3–4

An Indian blend of spices complements pasta and chicken in this savory dish.

1 1/2 cups macaroni or tubetti
3–4 tbs. butter
4 boneless, skinless chicken breast
  halves
1/4 cup minced green onions, including
  1 inch green part
1 clove garlic, minced
2 tbs. flour
1 can (14 1/2 oz.) chicken broth
1 cup sour cream
1/4 tsp. cinnamon

1/4 tsp. ground coriander
1/4 tsp. grated fresh ginger
1/4 tsp. pepper
1/4 tsp. cumin seed
1/2 tsp. ground cardamom
1/2 tsp. salt
1 tbs. soy sauce
1/4 tsp. Tabasco Sauce, or to taste
grated zest of 1 lemon
1/4 cup coarsely chopped dry-roasted
  peanuts for garnish

Heat oven to 350.° Cook pasta according to package directions.

Melt butter in a medium skillet. Sauté chicken breasts over medium heat for 3 to 4 minutes per side. Remove from skillet and set aside. Add green onions and garlic to pan. Cook for 1 to 2 minutes. Stir in flour and cook for 1 minute. Add chicken broth. Cook, stirring, until sauce thickens. Add remaining ingredients except peanuts. Mix well.

Pour hot, well-drained pasta into a buttered casserole. Place chicken breasts over pasta and top with sour cream sauce. Bake for 15 to 20 minutes, until bubbling. Garnish with peanuts. Serve immediately.

TURKEY, BROCCOLI AND NOODLE STIR-FRY

Preparation time: 30 minutes
Servings: 2–3

Cut a turkey tenderloin into thin slices across the grain for this dish. For a short-cut, cook the broccoli with the pasta for the last 5 minutes.

4 oz. dried pasta shapes (orecchiette or fusilli)
1 bunch broccoli florets, about 3 cups
8 oz. turkey tenderloin, cut into thin slices
1 tsp. dry sherry
1 tsp. soy sauce
1 tsp. cornstarch
3 tbs. vegetable oil, divided
4 green onions, thinly sliced
1/2-inch piece fresh ginger, peeled and minced
1 small clove garlic, minced
1/2 lb. mushrooms, thinly sliced
1/2 cup chicken broth
1/2 tsp. red pepper flakes
salt and freshly ground pepper to taste
1 tsp. cornstarch dissolved in 1 tbs. soy sauce

Heat pasta water. About 5 minutes before pasta has finished cooking, add broccoli to cooking water. Combine turkey slices, sherry, soy sauce and cornstarch and marinate while preparing remaining ingredients.

Heat 2 tbs. of the vegetable oil in a large nonstick skillet. Sauté onion, ginger and garlic over medium-high heat for 1 minute. Add mushrooms and cook for 2 to 3 minutes. Pour mushrooms out onto a plate. Add remaining vegetable oil to skillet and sauté turkey pieces for 2 to 3 minutes, stirring constantly. Return mushrooms to pan and add chicken broth, pepper flakes, salt and pepper. Bring to a boil.

Pour hot, well-drained pasta and broccoli into skillet with turkey and toss to combine. Bring sauce to a boil and add a small amount of dissolved cornstarch to thicken sauce just enough to coat meat. Serve immediately on warm plates.

SPICY PORK WITH NOODLES

Preparation time: 30 minutes
Servings: 6

Chicken or shrimp can be substituted for pork in this zesty stir-fry dish.

1 lb. thin fresh Hong Kong-style noodles
1½ lb. pork tenderloin
1½ tbs. cornstarch
2 tbs. soy sauce
2 tbs. dry sherry
7 tbs. vegetable oil, divided
1 lb. fresh mushrooms, sliced
6 green onions, thinly sliced
1 red, yellow or green bell pepper, coarsely chopped
1 clove garlic, minced
½ tsp. dried red pepper flakes, or to taste
2 cups chicken broth
1 tsp. toasted sesame oil
1 pkg. (10 oz. pkg.) peas, defrosted if frozen

Cook noodles according to package directions. Drain, fill pan with cool water and return noodles to pan.

Slice pork into 1/4-inch by 1-inch-long match-sticks. Combine sliced pork with cornstarch, soy sauce and sherry. Let stand for 10 to 15 minutes.

Heat 4 tbs. of the oil in a large skillet or wok. Sauté mushrooms for 4 to 5 minutes. Remove from skillet and set aside. Add remaining 3 tbs. oil in same skillet; when very hot, add marinated pork, green onions, pepper, garlic and red pepper flakes. Cook, stirring constantly, until pork is cooked. Lift mixture from skillet and pour off any remaining oil. Add chicken broth to skillet and bring to a boil, scraping brown bits from bottom of pan. Add mushrooms, pork mixture, sesame oil, peas and drained cooked noodles. Stir-fry for a few minutes, until ingredients are well combined and hot. Serve immediately in a large warm bowl.

SPICY LAMB RAGU

Preparation time: 20 minutes
Cooking time: 45 minutes
Servings: 3–4

This hearty sauce can be easily doubled and is great to have on hand in the refrigerator or freezer.

1 tbs. olive oil
3/4 cup chopped onion
1/4 tsp. red pepper flakes
1/2 lb. lean ground lamb
3 cloves garlic, coarsely chopped
1 1/2 tsp. dried marjoram
1/2 cup beef broth
1 can (14 1/2 oz.) ready-cut tomatoes
1 can (8 oz.) Italian style tomato sauce
1/2 tsp. salt
generous amounts freshly ground black pepper
1 lb. pappardelle or penne
grated pecorino cheese for garnish

In a large nonstick skillet, heat olive oil over medium heat and sauté onion for 6 to 8 minutes, until soft and translucent. Increase heat and add red pepper flakes, lamb and garlic. Break up lamb with a spatula and cook for about 5 minutes, until meat is lightly browned. Add marjoram and beef broth and bring to a boil. Add tomatoes, tomato sauce, salt and pepper. Reduce heat and simmer for 45 minutes, stirring occasionally to break up big pieces of meat. Sauce can be cooled and refrigerated or frozen at this point.

To serve, heat pasta water and cook pasta according to package directions. Pour drained pasta into skillet with hot sauce and gently toss to combine. Serve immediately on warm plates and pass Parmesan cheese.

Wine suggestion: red Zinfandel or Italian Barbera

PASTA WITH TURKEY AND RED PEPPERS

Preparation time: 30 minutes
Servings: 2–3

This recipe can be made quickly if you have cooked turkey or chicken on hand. Use fusilli or radiatore pasta to capture the delicious sauce.

6 oz. dried fusilli pasta
2 tbs. butter
1/2 cup chopped onion
1/2 lb. mushrooms, thinly sliced
1 medium red bell pepper, peeled
  and cut into 1/4-inch squares
1 1/2 cups diced cooked turkey

1/3 cup chicken broth
2 tbs. heavy cream
salt and freshly ground pepper to taste
1 dash red pepper flakes
grated Parmesan cheese
1 fresh tomato, peeled and chopped,
  for garnish

Bring pasta water to a boil. Cook pasta according to package directions. Melt butter in a large nonstick skillet. Sauté onion for 2 to 3 minutes to soften. Increase heat to medium-high and sauté mushrooms for 2 to 3 minutes. Add red pepper pieces, turkey, chicken broth, cream, salt, pepper and red pepper flakes. Cook for about 5 minutes, until sauce thickens. Add hot, well-drained pasta to skillet and toss with sauce to combine. Pour into a warm serving bowl and sprinkle with Parmesan cheese and fresh tomato pieces. Serve immediately on warm plates. Pass additional Parmesan cheese.

LINGUINE WITH SMOKED TURKEY AND TARRAGON

Preparation time: 20 minutes
Servings: 2–3

Smoked turkey or chicken strips make a rich -tasting pasta dish. Add some fresh tomato pieces for color just before serving.

4 oz. dried linguine,
  or 6 oz. fresh
2 tbs. butter
3 green onions, thinly sliced
2 medium carrots, cut into thin 2-inch
  x ¼-inch strips
2 tbs. chicken stock or dry white wine
2 tbs. heavy cream

½ tsp. dried tarragon
salt and freshly ground pepper to taste
4 oz. sliced smoked turkey, cut into
  thin 2-inch x ¼-inch pieces
1 medium tomato, peeled, seeded
  and chopped
grated Parmesan cheese

Bring pasta water to a boil. Heat butter in a large skillet. Sauté onions and carrots for 3 to 4 minutes, until onion softens. Add chicken stock, cream, tarragon, salt and pepper and simmer for 2 to 3 minutes. Pour hot, well-drained pasta into skillet. Add turkey pieces and toss to combine with sauce. Pour into a warm serving bowl, top with tomato pieces and serve immediately on warm plates. Pass the Parmesan cheese.

PASTA WITH ITALIAN SAUSAGE

Preparation time: 15 minutes
Cooking time: 30 minutes
Servings: 3–4

This is an excellent sauce to make ahead. While the pasta cooks, reheat the sauce in a large skillet. Try it with spaghetti or rigatoni.

12 oz. fresh pasta, or 8 oz. dried
4 mild or hot Italian sausages
1 small yellow onion, finely chopped
1 small bell pepper, finely chopped
1 can (28 oz.) ready-cut tomatoes with juice

$1/3$ cup dry red wine
2 tsp. dried oregano
salt and freshly ground pepper to taste
2 tbs. minced fresh flat-leaf parsley or basil
freshly grated Parmesan cheese

Heat pasta water and time pasta to be done when sauce is ready. Slit sausage casings and remove meat from casings. Flatten sausage meat to about $1/2$-inch. Place in a large cold skillet; heat and brown on both sides. Remove sausage meat from pan and chop coarsely. Pour out all but 2 tbs. of the fat and add onion and pepper to skillet. Cook over low heat for 3 to 4 minutes, until softened. Add tomatoes, sausage meat, wine, oregano, salt and pepper to skillet. Simmer uncovered for 25 to 30 minutes. Pour hot, well-drained pasta into sauce and combine. Add parsley. Serve immediately on heated plates. Pass Parmesan or Asiago cheese.

RAVIOLI

Ravioli are little pillows of flat pasta filled with meat, cheese, or other good things, and served with a sauce or just melted butter and cheese. There are many prepared kinds of ravioli available in the fresh pasta section of most supermarkets.

Ravioli can be quickly and easily made from won ton wrappers. The wrappers are available in squares and rounds, and a variety of sizes and thicknesses. Avoid the thickest won ton skins because they take a long time to cook and do not provide a melt-in-your mouth texture. Sandwich your filling between two squares or circles, or fold one wrapper into a triangular shape or crescent.

Ravioli fillings can be made with a wide variety of foods. Chicken, shrimp, clams, veal, sun-dried tomatoes, spinach and cheese, used alone or in combinations make good fillings. Some ravioli fillings tend to be very lightly seasoned so they are complemented with flavorful tomato sauces or pesto. Others need only a little melted butter and some Parmesan cheese to finish them perfectly.

To fill ravioli: If making triangles or crescents, spread about 1 to 1½ tsp. filling in the center of the won ton skin. Brush two adjacent edges with water. Carefully fold over the wrapper, firmly pressing the unmoistened edge to the moistened edge. Press out as much air as possible and firmly pinch the mating edges together. If making squares or rounds, place no more than 2 tsp. of filling in center of won ton, moisten all edges of won ton with filling, and press another won ton over filling, pressing down firmly around all edges. Edges of filled ravioli can be fluted with fork tines, or use a fluted ravioli cutter to make a decorative edge. Place on a rack and allow to dry for a few minutes before cooking.

To cook ravioli, add about 2 inches of water to a large skillet or shallow saucepan, and bring to a rapid boil. Add 2 tsp. salt. Reduce heat to a simmer and slide in ravioli. Gently cook for 5 to 6 minutes, depending on thickness of dough and size. Gently lift cooked ravioli from water with a flat strainer or large slotted spoon and drain well. Transfer to a heated bowl. Gently toss with hot sauce or melted butter and Parmesan cheese. Serve immediately on warm plates.

Here are several very easy and satisfying quick ravioli recipes. Try a couple of them and then make up your own fillings. Top with just butter and cheese, or purchase a container of tomato or pesto sauce from the deli case.

CHEESE FILLING FOR RAVIOLI

Preparation time: 30 minutes
Makes: 20–24 ravioli

This is a simple, classic cheese filling for ravioli. Mix it up ahead and refrigerate until you are ready to make the ravioli, or double the recipe if you want to make a larger batch. After cooking, serve with a sauce or gently toss with a little melted butter and some Parmesan cheese.

20–24 won ton wrappers
3/4 cup ricotta cheese
1/2 cup grated Parmesan cheese
2 tbs. minced fresh flat-leaf parsley
1 large egg

generous amount white pepper
1 dash nutmeg
salt to taste
1/2 tsp. grated lemon zest

SAUCE

3 tbs. butter, melted
additional grated Parmesan cheese

3 tbs. minced fresh flat-leaf parsley
1 tomato, peeled, seeded and chopped

Combine all filling ingredients in a small bowl. Mix until well combined. Refrigerate until needed to fill ravioli. Fill and cook ravioli as directed on pages 125–126. Place hot drained ravioli in a heated bowl. Pour hot melted butter over and add cheese, tomatoes and parsley or a prepared sauce of your choice. Toss gently to combine. Serve immediately on warm plates.

GOAT CHEESE AND SUN-DRIED TOMATO FILLING

Preparation time: 30 minutes
Makes: 20–24 ravioli

This savory filling needs only a little melted butter and a sprinkle of Parmesan cheese for a sauce. Four or five ravioli make a satisfying first course serving. Make the filling ahead and refrigerate until ready to use.

4 oz. fresh goat cheese
1/3 cup oil-packed sun-dried tomatoes,
   coarsely chopped
1 large egg
generous amounts freshly ground black
   pepper

1/2 tsp. dried oregano
1/4 cup grated Parmesan cheese
20–24 fresh won ton wrappers
3 tbs. butter, melted, for topping
grated Parmesan cheese for topping

Mix goat cheese, sun-dried tomatoes, egg, black pepper, oregano and Parmesan cheese. Fill and cook ravioli as directed on pages 125–126. Place hot, drained ravioli in a heated bowl. Pour hot melted butter over and gently turn to coat ravioli. Sprinkle with cheese and serve immediately on warm plates. Pass additional Parmesan cheese.

BLACK OLIVE PASTE AND RICOTTA RAVIOLI FILLING

Preparation time: 30 minutes
Makes: 20–24 ravioli

Here is a zesty, quick ravioli filling.

20–24 won ton wrappers
4 oz. ricotta
1 large egg
2 tbs. black olive paste
1/4 cup grated Parmesan cheese
2 tbs. finely chopped fresh flat-leaf parsley
2 tbs. finely chopped fresh basil
3 tbs. butter, melted
grated Parmesan cheese for topping

Combine ricotta, egg, black olive paste, cheese, parsley and basil in a small bowl. Fill and cook ravioli as directed on pages 125–126. Place hot, drained ravioli in a heated bowl, pour hot melted butter over, and gently toss to coat ravioli. Sprinkle with cheese and serve immediately on warm plates. Pass additional Parmesan cheese.

SWEET POTATO RAVIOLI FILLING

Preparation time: 30 minutes
Makes: 20–24 ravioli

Baked sweet potato or canned pumpkin makes a great savory ravioli stuffing and is complemented with a simple butter, pine nut and sage sauce.

20–24 won ton wrappers
1 tbs. butter
6 green onions, including 1 inch green part, thinly sliced
1 cup baked sweet potato pulp or canned pumpkin
1 pinch grated nutmeg
$\frac{1}{2}$ tsp. grated orange zest
salt and freshly ground black pepper to taste

SAUCE
3 tbs. butter
2 tbs. pine nuts
3 or 4 fresh sage leaves, finely chopped

Melt 1 tbs. butter in a medium skillet and sauté onions for 4 to 5 minutes, until soft. Add sweet potato, nutmeg, orange zest, salt and pepper and cook for 2 to 3 minutes, until mixture is quite dry. Remove from heat, spread out on a plate and let cool until lukewarm. Fill and cook ravioli as directed on pages 125–126.

To make sauce: Melt butter in a small skillet over medium heat and sauté pine nuts until golden brown. Add sage.

Place hot, drained, cooked ravioli in a heated bowl, pour hot butter sauce over and gently toss to coat the ravioli. Serve immediately on warm plates.

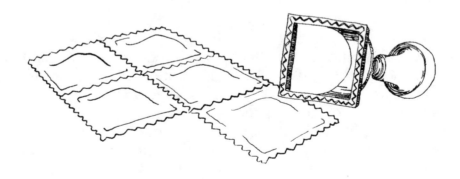

SHRIMP AND PEPPERED
CREAM CHEESE RAVIOLI FILLING

Preparation time: 30 minutes
Makes: 20–24 ravioli

Small salad shrimp and peppered cream cheese ravioli are sauced with a little butter and chopped tomato.

20–24 won ton wrappers
3/4 cup whipped cream cheese
1/2 tsp. coarsely ground black pepper

1 pinch cayenne pepper
40–48 small cooked salad shrimp,
　defrosted if frozen

SAUCE

3 tbs. butter
1 large tomato, peeled, seeded and
　chopped

salt and freshly ground black pepper

In a small bowl, combine cream cheese, black pepper and cayenne pepper and mix well. To fill ravioli, use about 1 tsp. of the cream cheese mixture for each won ton, placing it in center of wrapper. Top with 2 salad shrimp. Continue folding and cooking instructions as directed on pages 125–126.

To make sauce: Melt butter in a small skillet. Add tomato, salt and pepper. Place hot, drained, cooked ravioli in a heated bowl, pour hot sauce over and gently turn to coat the ravioli. Serve immediately on warm plates.

BAKED PASTA DISHES

Lasagna is taking on a new look with vegetables replacing the traditional meat and tomato sauce. No-cook or instant lasagna noodles are available and produce tender, delicate layers of pasta. These noodles can be soaked in hot water for 4 to 5 minutes and cut to form wrappers for ravioli or cannelloni. Chinese egg roll wrappers, about 6 inches square, also can be used for the fresh pasta in lasagna or cannelloni dishes if cooked in boiling water for about 2 minutes before using. Many markets sell fresh wide lasagna noodles in the refrigerator case which only need to be cooked briefly before assembling lasagna.

Included in this section are some favorite lasagna recipes. There is a zesty Swiss chard and black olive combination; shrimp and scallops folded into a lemony tarragon sauce and then layered with tender no-cook noodles for an elegant seafood lasagna; and asparagus and goat cheese used to fill cannelloni made from instant lasagna noodles. There are other baked dishes, too: manicotti; chicken and noodle casserole; and a good Armenian pilaf.

ORZO AND GREEN CHILE CASSEROLE

Preparation time: 15 minutes
Baking time: 20 minutes
Servings: 4

Cook the orzo and then fold in diced green chiles, cheese and sour cream and bake. This makes a delicious side dish to take to a barbecue or a potluck.

1/2 cup orzo or other small grain-shaped pasta
1/2 cup sour cream
1/2 cup grated sharp cheddar cheese
1 can (4 oz.) diced green chiles with liquid
2 small tomatoes, peeled, seeded and chopped
salt and freshly ground black pepper to taste

Heat oven to 375°. Cook pasta according to package directions. Drain and pour into an ovenproof baking dish. Stir in sour cream and grated cheese and fold in chiles and tomatoes. Top with Parmesan cheese. Bake for 20 to 25 minutes, until lightly browned and bubbling.

Variation: Substitute 4 oz. goat cheese and 1/3 cup diced sun-dried tomatoes for the cheddar cheese and green chiles.

SWISS CHARD AND BLACK OLIVE LASAGNA

Preparation time: 45 minutes
Baking time: 25 minutes
Servings: 3–4

Cover the instant lasagna noodles with hot water for 4 to 5 minutes to soften them before using in the recipe.

1 bunch Swiss chard, about 1 lb.
2 tbs. extra virgin olive oil
1 large onion, chopped
2 cloves garlic, minced
1 red bell pepper, peeled and diced
1 pkg. (00 oz.) instant lasagna noodles, softened in hot water

1 large egg
4 oz. ricotta cheese
1/2 tsp. dried thyme, or 1 tbs. fresh
3 tbs. black olive paste
freshly ground black pepper to taste
grated Parmesan cheese for topping
Bechamel Sauce, follows

Strip leaves from Swiss chard stems and discard stems. Chop leaves into 1-inch or smaller pieces. There will be about 4 cups. Heat olive oil in a large skillet. Add onion and sauté for 6 to 8 minutes, until onion softens. Add chard, garlic and red pepper. Continue to cook until all liquid has evaporated and chard has softened. Remove from heat and let cool before adding to ricotta mixture.

Prepare instant lasagna noodles by softening 4 large or 8 small pieces (to make 4 layers) in hot water for 3 to 4 minutes before using. If using fresh or traditional dried lasagna, cook according to package directions.

Beat egg lightly in a large bowl. Whisk in ricotta, thyme, black olive paste and generous grinds of black pepper. Add cooled chard mixture and $1/2$ cup of the bechamel. Stir to combine. Heat oven to 350°.

To assemble: Reserve 1 cup *Bechamel Sauce* for the top layer. Spread a thin layer of sauce in the bottom of an 8-inch-square baking pan. Cover with a layer of lasagna noodles. Spread about $1/3$ of the chard mixture over noodles and cover with about $1/3$ of the remaining sauce. Continue with another lasagna layer, chard and sauce, making 2 more layers. Finish with the last lasagna layer and spread with reserved cup of sauce. Sprinkle with Parmesan cheese. Cover with foil and bake for 15 minutes. Uncover and bake for another 10 minutes. If desired, run under the broiler to lightly brown the top. Allow to rest for 5 minutes before serving. Cut into squares and serve on warm plates. Lasagna can be assembled in advance and refrigerated. Cover and add an additional 15 minutes baking time if you assemble in advance.

BECHAMEL SAUCE

$1/4$ cup butter
3 tbs. flour
2 cups milk

salt and freshly ground pepper
$1/2$ cup Parmesan cheese
1 dash nutmeg

Melt butter in a small saucepan. Stir in flour and cook over low heat for 2 minutes. Gradually add milk and cook, stirring, until sauce thickens. Add remaining ingredients and cook for 3 or 4 minutes. Use as directed.

SEAFOOD LASAGNA

Preparation time: 30 minutes
Baking time: 20 minutes
Servings: 3–4 main course or 6 appetizers

Small bay scallops and shrimp folded into a creamy tarragon sauce are baked between tender lasagna noodles for an elegant first course or luncheon dish. Use the delicate no-boil or instant lasagna noodles, egg roll wrappers (cooked for 2 minutes), or cooked, very thin, fresh homemade pasta. The traditional ruffle-edged lasagna noodles are too thick for this preparation.

1 pkg. no-cook or instant lasagna noodles for 5 layers, softened in hot water for 4–5 minutes

$1/2$ lb. uncooked small bay scallops

$1/2$ lb. uncooked small peeled, deveined shrimp

$1/3$ cup grated mozzarella or Monterey Jack cheese

SAUCE

3 tbs. butter

2 tbs. finely chopped shallots

3 tbs. flour

1 cup clam juice

$1 1/2$ cups light cream

1 tsp. Dijon mustard

2 tbs. lemon juice

$1/2$ tsp. dried tarragon

salt and generous amount white pepper

Heat oven to 350°. Prepare scallops by removing small white muscle and rinsing well to remove any sand. Peel and devein shrimp. Cut small shrimp in half lengthwise. If using larger shrimp, cut into same size pieces as scallops.

To make sauce: Melt butter in a small saucepan. Sauté shallots for 1 to 2 minutes to soften. Add flour and cook for 1 to 2 minutes. Whisk in clam juice and cream, bring to a boil and cook until sauce thickens. Stir in mustard, lemon juice, tarragon, salt and white pepper. Reserve ¾ cup of the sauce for topping.

To assemble: Cover bottom of an 8-inch square baking pan with a thin layer of sauce. Fold uncooked seafood into remaining hot sauce. Place a lasagna layer on top of sauce in pan. Top with about ¼ of the seafood mixture. Continue layering lasagna squares and sauce to make 3 more layers. Top with last lasagna piece. Spread with reserved sauce and sprinkle with grated cheese. Cover with foil and bake for 20 minutes, until heated through. Broil for 1 to 2 minutes to melt cheese and lightly brown top. Allow to stand for 5 minutes before serving. There will be a little extra sauce in bottom of baking pan to spoon over served portions. Cut into squares and serve on warm plates.

Serving suggestion: a crisp Chardonnay or Pinot Grigio

VEGETABLE LASAGNA

Preparation time: 1 hour
Baking time: 25 minutes
Servings: 4–5

This dish takes a while to put together ,but it can be assembled a day in advance and baked before serving.

Tomato Sauce, follows
Vegetable Sauce, follows
1 pkg fresh, traditional dried, or
   instant lasagna noodles, cooked
   according to pkg. directions (enough
   for 4 layers)

2 cups ricotta cheese
1/2 cup grated Parmesan cheese

Prepare *Tomato Sauce* and *Vegetable Sauce*. Heat oven to 350°. Place one layer lasagna noodles in a buttered 9-x-13-inch baking dish. Cover with 1/2 of the vegetable sauce. Spread 1/2 cup of the ricotta cheese over vegetable layer. Cover with another layer of noodles. Repeat vegetable and ricotta cheese layers. Pour about 1/3 cup of the tomato sauce over ricotta. Top with final layer of lasagna noodles. Spread with remaining ricotta cheese. Distribute remaining tomato sauce over cheese and top with Parmesan cheese. Bake for 20 to 25 minutes, until hot and bubbly. Let stand for 10 minutes before cutting into serving pieces.

TOMATO SAUCE

1 can (15 oz.) tomato puree
1 tsp. dried basil
1 tsp. dried oregano

2 tbs. dry white wine or dry vermouth
freshly ground black pepper to taste

Combine all ingredients in a small saucepan. Bring to a boil and simmer, uncovered, over medium heat for 10 minutes.

VEGETABLE SAUCE

$1/3$ cup extra virgin olive oil
1 cup finely chopped onion
$1/4$–$1/2$ tsp. hot red pepper flakes
1 lb. mushrooms, coarsely chopped
2 cloves garlic, minced
2 cups coarsely grated carrots

1 red bell pepper, finely chopped
1 green bell pepper, finely chopped
$1 1/2$ cups peeled, diced eggplant
salt and freshly ground black pepper
   to taste

Heat olive oil in a large skillet. Add onion and pepper flakes; sauté for 5 to 6 minutes, until onions are soft but not browned. Increase heat and add mushrooms. Sauté for 3 to 4 minutes. Add garlic, carrots, bell pepper, eggplant, salt and pepper and sauté for 3 to 4 minutes. Cover pan and cook over low heat for about 15 minutes.

Wine suggestion: Sauvignon blanc or rosé

ASPARAGUS AND GOAT CHEESE CANNELLONI

Preparation time: 30 minutes
Makes: 10 cannelloni

Instant lasagna noodles are stuffed with a savory goat cheese filling and green asparagus tips and baked with a creamy dill sauce. Soften the pasta by soaking in hot water for 3 to 4 minutes, and then cut it into squares. If you have thick asparagus, use only one per cannelloni.

10 thick or 20 thin asparagus tips
10 softened instant lasagna noodles, cut about 4 inches square

FILLING

1 tbs. minced shallots
1 tbs. lemon juice
4 oz. goat cheese

1 large egg
$1/2$ tsp. Dijon mustard
2 tbs. grated Parmesan cheese

CREAMY DILL SAUCE

2 tbs. butter
2 tbs. flour
$1 1/2$ cups milk
$1/2$ tsp. Worcestershire sauce

1 tbs. finely chopped fresh dill, or
    1 tsp. dried dill weed
salt and freshly ground pepper to taste
$3/4$ cup grated Gruyère cheese

To make filling: Microwave shallots with lemon juice for about 1 minute on high power. Let cool. In a small bowl combine remaining filling ingredients; beat until smooth and creamy. Add cooled shallot mixture to filling.

To make sauce: Melt butter in a small saucepan, add flour and cook for 2 minutes. Gradually add milk, stirring to make a smooth sauce. Cook over medium heat until sauce thickens and comes to a boil. Add Worcestershire, dill, salt, pepper and $1/2$ of the Gruyère cheese. Stir until combined. Remove from heat and cool slightly before using.

Snap tough ends from asparagus spears. The asparagus pieces should be just a little longer than the pasta squares. Cook asparagus in boiling water for about 5 minutes, drain and cover with cold water to stop cooking process.

To assemble: Heat oven to 350°. Spread a thin layer of sauce in the bottom of an 8-inch-square baking pan. Spread a pasta square with a thin layer of filling, spreading to edges. Place 2 asparagus spears at one end of pasta and roll up. Place seam side down in baking pan. Assemble rest of cannelloni. Top with remaining cheese sauce. Sprinkle with remaining grated Gruyère. Cover with foil and bake for 20 minutes until cannelloni are bubbling hot. Uncover and run under the broiler to lightly brown the top.

MANICOTTI STUFFED WITH
BROCCOLI AND CANADIAN BACON

Preparation time: 30 minutes
Baking time: 15 minutes
Servings: 4

Stuffed pasta tubes (manicotti) are arranged in an oven-to-table serving dish to make an attractive buffet or potluck main course.

8 manicotti tubes
1 tbs. butter
4 green onions, including 1 inch green part, thinly sliced
1 cup diced Canadian bacon or cooked ham
1 cup ricotta cheese
$1/4$ cup grated Parmesan cheese
1 large egg
salt and freshly ground pepper to taste
2 cups coarsely chopped cooked broccoli

CHEESE SAUCE

3 tbs. butter
3 tbs. flour
2 cups milk

$1/2$ tsp. Worcestershire sauce
$3/4$ cup grated Swiss or Gruyère cheese
salt and freshly ground pepper to taste

To make sauce: Melt butter in a small saucepan. Add flour and cook, stirring, for 2 minutes. Gradually add milk and Worcestershire sauce. Cook, stirring constantly, until sauce thickens. Add cheese, salt and pepper. Stir to blend.

Heat oven to 350°. Cook manicotti tubes according to package directions. Drain and rinse in cold water for easier handling. Melt butter in a small skillet and sauté onions for 1 to 2 minutes to soften. Add Canadian bacon pieces and cook for 1 to 2 minutes. In a small bowl, combine ricotta, Parmesan cheese, egg, salt and pepper. Mix well. Add bacon mixture, chopped broccoli and $\frac{1}{2}$ cup of the cheese sauce and combine. Use a teaspoon to stuff tubes with filling. Place stuffed manicotti in a buttered ovenproof baking dish or in individual au gratin dishes. Spoon remaining cheese sauce over shells. Bake for 15 minutes, until hot and bubbly. Place under broiler to brown lightly. Serve on warm plates.

WALNUT CHICKEN AND NOODLE CASSEROLE

Preparation time: 30 minutes
Baking time: 20 to 25 minutes
Servings: 4–6

Crunchy walnuts add an interesting texture to this creamy noodle casserole.

12 oz. fresh wide noodles or linguine, or 8 oz. dried
7 tbs. butter, divided
5 tbs. flour
3 cups chicken broth
1/3 cup dry sherry or white wine
1/2 tsp. paprika

salt and freshly ground pepper to taste
8 oz. mushrooms, thinly sliced
2–2 1/2 cups diced cooked chicken or turkey
1/2 cup coarsely chopped toasted walnuts
grated Parmesan cheese

Heat oven to 350°. Cook pasta, drain well and place in a large buttered casserole. Melt 5 tbs. butter in a saucepan. Add flour and cook, stirring, for 2 minutes. Gradually add chicken broth, sherry, paprika, salt and pepper. Cook, stirring constantly, until sauce thickens. Melt remaining butter in a medium skillet. Sauté mushrooms for 4 to 5 minutes. Combine mushrooms, chicken and walnuts with pasta in casserole. Add sauce, mix carefully and top with Parmesan cheese. Bake for 20 to 25 minutes, until hot and bubbly. Serve on warm plates.

Wine suggestion: Sauvignon blanc or dry Riesling

ARMENIAN PILAF

Preparation time: 15 minutes
Baking time: 30 minutes
Servings: 4–6

This classic pilaf goes perfectly with lamb shish kabob.

3 cans (14½ oz. each) chicken broth
8 tbs. butter, divided
½ cup crushed dried fine egg noodles
2 cups uncooked long-grain rice

Heat oven to 350°. Bring chicken broth to a boil in a saucepan. Melt 4 tbs. of the butter in a 3-quart flameproof casserole or ovenproof pan with a tightly fitting lid. Add crushed noodles to melted butter and stir until lightly browned. Add boiling broth and rice. Stir gently. Boil for 5 minutes. Cover casserole and place in oven. Bake for 20 to 25 minutes, or until all liquid is absorbed. Stir gently and dot with remaining butter. Return to oven and bake uncovered for 5 minutes. Serve immediately.

PASTA SHAPES

Agnolotti - Small crescent-shaped ravioli, often stuffed with a meat filling.

Anellini - Little rings. Can be baked in sauce or added to soups.

Angel Hair - "Capelli D'Angelo." Long, very thin strands. Because of their delicacy best served with light sauces.

Bucatini - Hollow long pasta tubes, a little thicker than spaghetti.

Cannelloni - Large tubes or squares of sheet pasta, stuffed, rolled into cylinders, sauced and baked.

Capellini - Thin round pasta, slightly thicker than angel hair.

Conchiglie - Also called "sea shells." Fluted shell-shaped pasta either ridged or smooth. The larger sizes can be stuffed and baked.

Ditali - Small, very short tubes of macaroni.

Farfalle - Butterfly- or bowtie-shaped pasta, available in many sizes.

Fettuccine - Ribbon noodles about $1/4$ inch wide, served with a wide variety of sauces, the most familiar being fettuccine Alfredo.

Fusilli - Corkscrew-shaped pasta, holds sauce well.

Gemellini - Hollow tubes twisted around each other and cut into 1½-inch lengths.

Lasagna - A wide flat noodle baked in layers with cheese and meat or vegetable filling.

Linguine - Spaghetti, slightly flattened into an oval shape.

Macaroni - Maccheroni is the Italian word for all pasta. The common usage means pasta tubes, often curved, which can be short, long, thick, thin or straight.

Manicotti - Either a large 4-inch-long, 1-inch-diameter tube, or a square of flat pasta which is stuffed, rolled into a cylinder, sauced and baked. Usually larger than cannelloni.

Mostaccioli - Almost identical to penne.

Noodles - Thin ribbons of flat pasta, usually containing eggs, available in widths from ⅛-inch to over 1 inch.

Orecchiette - Small ear-shaped pieces of pasta.

Orzo - Small pointed rice grain-shaped pasta, usually used in soups.

Pappardelle - Very thin 1-inch or wider strips of pasta. Often served with ragout of game.

Pastina - General term for the whole group of tiny pasta varieties including alphabets, stars and riso that are usually used in soup.

Penne - Tubular pasta, sometimes ridged, with ends cut at an angle. Good with rich sauces or in baked dishes.

Radiatore - "Little radiators." A newer shape, with numerous ridges to hold sauce. Dense and compact. Does well with hearty sauces.

Ravioli - A well-known square pasta dumpling stuffed with various meat, cheese or vegetable fillings.

Rigatoni - Hollow ridged straight macaroni tubes about $1/2$ inch in diameter by 2 inches long.

Rotelle - Small spoked wagon wheel-shaped pasta.

Spaghetti - Thin, solid round pasta strings, any length.

Spirali - Corkscrew-shaped pasta. Pretty in salads.

Tagliatelle - Long thin flat egg noodles, ranging from $1/4$ inch to $1/2$ inches wide.

Tortellini - Small ring or half-moon-shaped stuffed pasta. Available both dried and fresh.

Tubetti - Short tubular pasta, also known as salad macaroni.

Vermicelli - Alternate name for spaghetti in Southern Italy, especially around Naples.

Ziti - A smaller and smoother type of rigatoni.

INDEX

Serve Creative, Easy, Nutritious Meals with nitty gritty® Cookbooks

100 Dynamite Desserts
The 9 x 13 Pan Cookbook
The Barbecue Cookbook
Beer and Good Food
The Best Bagels are Made at Home
The Best Pizza is Made at Home
The Big Book of Bread Machine
  Recipes
Blender Drinks
Bread Baking
Bread Machine Cookbook
Bread Machine Cookbook II
Bread Machine Cookbook III
Bread Machine Cookbook V
Bread Machine Cookbook VI
The Little Burger Bible
Cappuccino/Espresso
Casseroles
The Coffee Book
Convection Oven Cookery
The Cook-Ahead Cookbook
Cooking for 1 or 2
Cooking in Clay

Cooking in Porcelain
Cooking on the Indoor Grill
Cooking with Chile Peppers
Cooking with Grains
Cooking with Your Kids
New Recipes for your Deep Fryer
The Dehydrator Cookbook
Edible Pockets for Every Meal
Entrees from Your Bread Machine
Extra-Special Crockery Pot Recipes
Fabulous Fiber Cookery
Fondue and Hot Dips
Fresh Vegetables
From Freezer, 'Fridge and Pantry
From Your Ice Cream Maker
The Garlic Cookbook
Healthy Cooking on the Run
Healthy Snacks for Kids
The Juicer Book
The Juicer Book II
Lowfat American Favorites
New International Fondue Cookbook
No Salt, No Sugar, No Fat

One-Dish Meals
The Pasta Machine Cookbook
Pinch of Time: Meals in Less than 30
  Minutes
Quick and Easy Pasta Recipes
Recipes for the Loaf Pan
Recipes for the Pressure Cooker
Risottos, Paellas, and other Rice
  Specialties
Rotisserie Oven Cooking
New Recipes for Your Sandwich Maker
The Sensational Skillet: Sautés and
  Stir-Fries
Slow Cooking in Crock-Pot,® Slow
  Cooker, Oven and Multi-Cooker
Soups and Stews
Tapas Fantasticas
The Toaster Oven Cookbook
Unbeatable Chicken Recipes
The Vegetarian Slow Cooker
New Waffles and Pizzelles
Wraps and Roll-Ups

For a free catalog, call: Bristol Publishing Enterprises.
(800) 346-4889
www.bristolpublishing.com